# REBECCA VIZARD
# ONCE UPON A PILLOW

## A STORY OF HOME, DESIGN, AND EXQUISITE TEXTILES

PHOTOGRAPHS BY ANTOINE BOOTZ

FOREWORD BY NEWELL TURNER

POINTED LEAF PRESS
WWW.POINTEDLEAFPRESS.COM

# JOHNSON'S
## PLANTATION, SECTION AND TOWNSHIP
# MAP
### OF
# TENSAS
### PARISH
# LOUISIANA.

SHOWING THE SEVERAL

**WARDS, ROADS, LEVEES AND FERRIES,**

AND THE CHANGE IN THE RIVER SINCE 1828.

AUTHORITIES

TITLE DEEDS, AND THE SURVEYS OF THE UNITED STATES, WITH SUCH CHANGES
AND ADDITIONS AS HAVE BEEN DISCOVERED BY SUBSEQUENT
SURVEYS AND RELIABLE INVESTIGATIONS TO
THE PRESENT DATE

### 1878

# Foreword

Few people or places in the United States embrace the Old World and its traditions the way Southerners do, especially in the lands along the Lower Mississippi River, where Spanish and French Catholics established themselves first. This temperate—tropical for much of the year—land proved fertile ground for their culture, with lavish sensibilities and tastes. While the early search for gold and silver in North America proved elusive, fertile ancient river deltas offered up unexpected new wealth from sugar cane, indigo, rice and cotton plantations—resources that fueled a passion for luxurious lifestyles, including houses furnished with Europe's finest decorative arts, crystal, porcelain and exquisite textiles.

The English, and in quick succession Americans, were not far behind settling among the French and Spanish, adopting their trappings of wealth and success. The complicated and dark tradition of slavery also took root, which eventually led to rebellion, followed by defeat, in the devastating Civil War. Fortunes evaporated, but a reverence for fine goods endured. New estates didn't materialize seemingly overnight, as they once had from one season's crops, so families religiously cherished what survived, passing down furnishings from one generation to the next. An appreciation, even lust, for the baroque also survived in interior decoration, and through events like debutante balls and carnivals, the most famous being New Orleans' opulent-to-excess Mardi Gras pageants, with their extraordinary costumes.

There are still many rural places across the United States, but there's an especially intense rural-ness to the Deep South. The land is always trying to return to wilderness, and houses in all their finery have long served as beacons of civilization along the snaking banks of old rivers and endless humid fields.

My friend Becky Vizard and I are from a delta that straddles the river between her Louisiana and my Mississippi. And we both share a love of textiles and their ability to elevate a room, giving it not only color and texture, but a sense of history. We see textiles as the world's cultural treasures, and we are equally passionate about the old mills and workshops still weaving legendary fabrics—especially the mysterious workshops of Fortuny in Venice where the dyeing techniques are still a secret. But Becky's obsession runs deeper, as a collector of vintage embroideries, appliqués, tapestry fragments, and needlepoint pieces to which she gives new life as pillows and decorative elements, enabling their rich stories to add a layer of complexity in the art of interior design.

In the South, we all love a good tale, especially one richly embellished, and there are amazing stories in the unique textiles and needlework for which Becky searches the world. In her hands, and in the hands of the lovely ladies of her small town who work with her to transform them into something new, the "lost stories" are not forgotten. They live for future generations to know.

Newell Turner, Editorial Director, Hearst Design Group
*Elle Decor / House Beautiful / Veranda*

**OPPOSITE** An antique 1878 map shows the Mississippi River, and the horse-shoe shape of Lake Bruin, which at one time was a curve in the mighty river.

**ABOVE** An 18th century distressed metallic appliqué on a watery pale French blue velvet captures the mood of the lake on a foggy morning.

**OPPOSITE** Cypress trees with Spanish moss are reflected in the calm water on a foggy morning, reminding me that where I live is like another world.

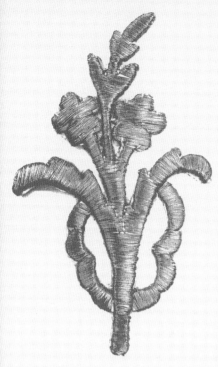

## Le Pecq, France
## April 13, 2015

Once upon the time I was resting on a stool at Vanves, the weekly Paris antiques market, when I noticed one of three nice American young ladies was embarrassed to explain in French what she was trying to purchase—our glances crossed and our friendship began.

Becky was launching her business to create pillows, the best of the best research for beautiful, unusual textiles and embroideries. It is more than half a century that I am wandering around and now am happy to introduce Becky to some dealers of antiques. Our priority was to find some more exceptional items to surprise the beauty of the following collection.

Becky was telling me how hard was the beginning and how wonderful it was when the first successes gave her a tremendous new energy with which she was able to move mountains.

I became so involved in Becky's research that I became very interested in discovering the first results.

In August 2003, another American friend and myself went to Louisiana invited by Becky and her husband to their lovely house Locustland on the edge of a sparkling lake of nature. How can I describe my surprise when Becky showed us some pillows. The only words are "full success"—of originality, imagination, harmony of lines, and colors. I also met Belinda, Becky's precious assistant.

During our collaboration, I noticed in Becky two qualities, extremely rare combined in one person: the artistic sensibility and the business skills.

From the bottom of my heart of a true friend I say "Bravo."

Marina TOSINI

**OPPOSITE** With Marina, in her antiques-filled cottage in Saint-Germain-en-Laye, outside Paris in 2015, we admired an 18th-century brocade that we decided was too delicate to be made into a pillow.

**OVERLEAF** The naked cotton field near my house is catching its breath before it erupts into a snowy frenzy in the fall. I love how, in the winter, the rows lend a striped pattern to the landscape.

19

The give and take of the universe has so seduced me that I love where I live, and I love where my business takes me. The two worlds could not be more different, yet they are both rich in diverse ways.

# Welcome to my world

I'm going to tell you about my little pillow-making business, but first you need to know a bit about me and where I live. I'm from the South, and we Southerners like to introduce ourselves before we try to sell you stuff. It's like in Istanbul, where you can't buy anything from a vendor until they serve you tea. We Southerners are overly polite that way.

If you were coming to visit me, you would probably fly into the Louis Armstrong New Orleans International Airport, then, if law abiding, drive *four* hours north. (For me, it's just a little over three.) When you think that it can't possibly be any farther, you come to a massive grey bridge—just like the one kids used to make with Erector Sets when they thought they wanted to grow up to be engineers. It's very nice. That churning muddy water you see below is the mighty Mississippi River. If you are very lucky you will see a paddlewheel boat; if not, you can buy a postcard from Natchez. Crossing the bridge, you are leaving Natchez where, in 1859, there were more millionaires per capita than anywhere in the United States (according to all the tour guides in their antebellum hoop skirts). The hilly terrain of Mississippi is behind you as you drive into the flatlands of Louisiana. This is where the working plantations generated the money to build many of those beautiful pre-Civil War mansions in Natchez. You'll drive through Ferriday, home of Jerry Lee Lewis, the legendary pioneer of rock 'n' roll. Known for his wild piano performances and his scandalous marriage to his 13-year-old cousin. (*Goodness Gracious, Great Balls of Fire!*) Keep going north. You are getting closer. Everyone who visits is advised to slow down about fifteen miles north of Ferriday, in a little town called Waterproof. Because of the area's poverty the one-tenth of a mile speed trap is more prosperous than the town's tax base. You will be entering a part of the United States called the Delta. The soil is rich, but the general population is not.

In his expedition notes, Hernando de Soto, the 16th-century Spanish explorer, marveled at this area's huge Indian population. (And unfortunately introduced European diseases, which decimated these early American inhabitants.) The land is so bountiful, and the rivers and bayous provided easy access for transportation and trade. Unfortunately, as transportation improved, the interstates bypassed us, the Mississippi River paddleboats became tourist rides, and our little part of the world kind of fell off the map. 'Way before my time the river even changed course, but luckily we were left with a beautiful remnant called Lake Bruin. It is a lovely, peaceful, horseshoe-shaped reservoir. (We like to call it environmental Prozac.) And don't forget, the land is still bountiful, so you see miles and miles of farmland.

But let's get back to your road trip. Keep going north for a few more miles and you'll turn right onto the crunch of the narrow Locustland gravel road. There are a lot of gravel roads around here, but this one will have a pecan orchard on your right and a cotton field on your left. You can tell the seasons of the year by this field. Right now it's winter, so you see shades of taupe when it's dry, but after a rain it becomes a rich dark chocolate, with puddles that reflect the sky. Spring is that same color but with light green stripes of the emerging plants. By summer, the field is a solid mass of rich green cotton plants, and in the fall, millions of white cotton bolls burst open, creating a snowy vista. The surrounding pecan trees are still a vivid green, with limbs sagging under the weight of the ripening pecans. We have more pecan trees in a 40-acre field across the main road. Perhaps my love of the leafy foliage of verdure tapestries comes from being surrounded by greenery for so much of the year.

Today we are shrouded in a heavy fog, and the nuances of color from the taupe winter field to the greys of the mist are truly breathtaking. I'm getting inspired to design pillows in silvery greys. Sorry, I got lost in my thoughts and left you down the way. As you near the end of the gravel road, our house is hidden behind overgrown azaleas and a mammoth live oak. That tree used to be full of dreamy hanging Spanish moss, but

**OPPOSITE** In early spring, as the first new leaves of the grand live oak emerge, the azaleas begin to put on their show. We built Locustland, our home, in 1989, on my grandfather's property. I remember telling our architect that I wanted a New Orleans-style farmhouse, lake house, and hunting lodge. He just laughed at me, but I think we got it.

this was my grandfather's property, and he was a bit of a neatnik. I don't know how he got rid of it, but it couldn't have been easy. You can better see the little house we call The Playhouse to the left, which was moved here from Cross Keys Plantation, where my Aunt Lucille lived. We passed the site of the old homestead on the way between Waterproof and here. But you can't see it from the road because it's hidden behind the trees on the banks of Lake St. Peter. This marsh is a very shallow, ancient oxbow lake that is good for duck hunting, and in 1847 gave Cross Keys its name. (St. Peter is the one who holds the keys to heaven.)

When the kids were on summer break from elementary school, and I was trying to get some design work done, I would bribe them with trips to Cross Keys if they let me finish. We would go out to the little bridge over the quiet bayou leading into Lake St. Peter and clap for the clapping gator, as there was this big alligator that would come when you clapped. I know it sounds absurd, but it's true. You can't make that kind of stuff up. Just ask my kids. I think he became trained by people who threw leftover fried chicken over the bridge. After a couple of years he mysteriously disappeared and I had to come up with a new bribery plan.

Let me get back on track and tell you about the Playhouse. It was built by servicemen in World War II because Aunt Lucille loved to open her home to those who wanted to hunt, fish, play poker, and relax when on leave. Ten years after she died, the original plantation house was struck by lightning and, to our horror, burned to the ground. The Playhouse sat uninhabited for another ten years, until Hurricane Katrina helped us realize we needed more evacuation space for our New Orleans relatives and friends. We were ever so happy to save it and move it to our property. The more this labor of love went over budget, the more certain I became that we would not have a hurricane for some time. So far so good.

The Playhouse is a real jewel. One of the soldiers was an artist and painted delightful ducks, frogs, and fish on the dark bourbon-colored boards of the main room. When you walk into this vintage structure, you can just feel the camaraderie and spirit of souls from a former era. The smoky smell of the fireplace along with a sweet essence of whiskey brings back childhood memories of Aunt Lucille barbecuing chicken for huge cocktailing crowds on Sunday afternoons. I wish I could bottle that scent.

If you walk back out of The Playhouse, you'll see our front door. But don't go there. No one uses that little porch. Instead, meander through the maze of gravel paths and plantings until you get to the door to the breezeway. The breezeway is full of gardening prints and objects of curiosity from nature, including a fig ivy vine that sneaked in through a crack. For years, I loved to watch that vine green up in the spring and creep across the tongue and groove ceiling when no one was looking. One dismal day, our gardener whacked it off at the root. I've left the delicate tracery of that dead vine there to remind me that you can't control either Mother Nature...or the gardener.

The enclosed breezeway is also the loading dock for my pillow business. The studio is to the right and the entrance to our house is to the left. The lake is 30 yards in front of you, just past the cutting garden. Behind you is the gravel road, cotton field, and pecan orchard. But let's go left into the original house that we built in 1989 with old salvaged pieces of wood, many from my grandfather's former fishing camp. Granddaddy used remnants of the original Locustland Plantation home when building his camp. (I suppose recycling and repurposing is in my blood.)

You will walk through our gallery of artworks and photographs. I especially love the one of Aunt Lucille standing on her horse. (Did I mention I come from a long line of characters?) As the hallway opens up, you'll see the kitchen, the real heart of the house. My adorable and fun-loving husband Michael is from a big family of cooking geniuses and fortunately he has the same cooking genius genes. He is always experimenting around the huge scarred and dappled antique pine table that came from a Parisian restaurant kitchen. The rest of the room looks like a mad scientist's laboratory, including the refrigerator of fame that is wallpapered with snapshots of family and friends. You'll also see a lovely antique door that hides a

**OPPOSITE** Lucille, our Brittany Spaniel, and Lou, my dad's Beagle, look smart with their B.Viz Canine Couture dog collars made of Fortuny fabric.

**OVERLEAF** The screened-in porch is our favorite place to dine. Suzani and kuba cloth pillows brighten the space. Lucille and Lou will be dashing through the doggie doors any minute now.

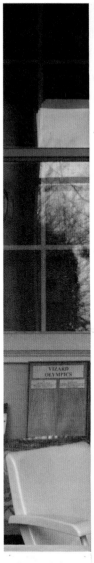

**LEFT** Suzani pillows warm the metal porch glider and rocking chairs that came from my Aunt Lucille's plantation. Our son Ross made the cross for me out of driftwood from the lake bank one Mother's Day morning, when he was empty-handed and wanted to give me a gift.

**OPPOSITE** Detail of a once-black and red suzani pillow that has faded to perfection in the strong Delta sun.

massive pantry. (Your pantry has to be sizeable if you are living in the middle of nowhere.) This cavern was also going to be our storm shelter, but now it is so packed with Michael's canned garden harvests that we are more liable to be killed by a head injury from tornado winds hurling mason jars of pickles—delicious but deadly missiles.

If you turn your back to the kitchen, you'll see our breakfast room, with the lake spread out perfectly through the French doors. It's lovely, but we prefer to go through the side French doors to the screened porch, and eat our meals there. Many evenings have been spent dining and telling stories around the long wood-topped iron table out here. If the kitchen is the heart of the house, the screen porch is its main artery. In Louisiana you can use a screened porch year-round. In the hottest part of the summer, we might add an extra fan, and we have a heater for unusually cold times in the winter. But most of the year, it is an absolutely delightful refuge. The grey-green colors, with their weathered patinas, are very relaxing and comfortable. There is something about patina that can just take the edge off. It's as if Mother Nature is telling you to loosen up. It's out of your control, so pay attention and see what beauty I can perform that you didn't think of. You can learn a lot from my friend Patina.

I love the sounds of the porch, where two doggie doors are constantly flapping and the hum of paws thump merrily on the wooden boards. Lucille, our Brittany Spaniel (named after Aunt Lucille, and B.B. King's guitar) and Lou, my dad's Beagle, have the run of the place. My 81-year-old dad, Bill Watson, lives next door. Lou and Lucille have the most wonderful life, dashing back and forth between our homes, treeing squirrels, and swimming in the lake. Actually we all do the same, except the treeing squirrels part.

Speaking of the lake, we don't have marinas to keep boats there. Everyone has a dock in their front yard that juts out into the lake. It's very handy to just walk down to the boathouse and flip a switch to lower the boat into the water. I could take the kids skiing or inner tubing after school, which was another great bribery tactic for getting homework done. Then we'd all jump in and wash our hair.

At night you can watch the moon rise over the lake and there is nothing more beautiful than a big orange harvest moon inching up over the cypress trees and reflecting on the water. That moon has instigated some crazy nights, when combined with guests. The scored concrete patio in front of the porch makes an excellent dance floor. We have had some times we'll never forget—and some we would like to forget. I won't name names...you know who you are.

If you go left of the porch toward my dad's house, you'll find a courtyard surrounded by azaleas and canopied with ancient live oaks, and a huge cypress tree that sashays in the lake breezes. The white Adirondack chairs circling the fire pit make another great spot to roost.

Just past the courtyard is the giant live oak that once bore the treehouse that was the pride and joy of our little carpenter son, Ross. We christened it Fort Eyesore. Fortunately, it was later dismantled with no serious injuries and we now have a sturdy tree swing hanging on the same limb that miraculously never betrayed our son—or at least not that I heard about.

Now back through the screen door to the porch—watch out for the dogs: They are eager to leap ahead through their own entrance, and turn back to make sure you are still with them. Take a right through one of the four sets of French doors into the big room with the wide cypress barn-board walls. I painted this room red after a trip to Paris when I became enamored with all the red lampshades I encountered. This was back before the internet, and after a year of looking for that European-style shade, I momentarily went insane and painted it red with a two-inch artist's brush. (This was when I was still having a bit of angst about living here.) My dear traveling partner, Ann Connelly, said, "That is entirely too aggressive a color for your personality." She was totally right, so I hired someone to come in and glaze the walls with raw sienna to tone them down. Now I absolutely love the room in the winter, though it feels hot as Hades in the summer. Although that

**OPPOSITE** The live oak that stands between our house and my dad's was the original structure for Fort Eyesore, the first somewhat-successful treehouse my son built. Now its beautiful silhouette, with a weathered porch swing, makes an unexpected backdrop for two pillows made from very old tapestry fragments. The human figure and the architectural column are two of my favorite tapestry subject matters.

**OVERLEAF** The view of Lake Bruin from the end of the dock provides a calm, peaceful, and contemplative feeling in the winter. As soon as daylight savings time starts, the lake begins to hum with the boats of ambitious fishermen and fearless water skiers.

**PAGES 38–39** The reflection of the ripples around a cypress tree seems to reflect the depth and watery characteristics of a vintage Fortuny Carnavalet design.

**PREVIOUS PAGES** The colors in the bark of the 65-year-old crepe myrtle down by the lake bank were the inspiration for the living room. The same glow of the crepe myrtle translates into reddish barn boards, a grunge green settee, a deerskin, and a pop of pink in an Ottoman Empire embroidered pillow.

**LEFT AND OPPOSITE** The bar links the kitchen to the warm barn-board living room. A 17th century or possibly earlier Italian fragment of an ionic column that I found in France has been mounted on homespun linen and framed for conservation purposes.

**OVERLEAF** The living room has been furnished with a bevy of antique textile pillows. The lamp bases have been made from Gulf of Mexico Oyster shells. The chandelier was created with wine corks and is a B.Viz Design project, to help create job opportunities in our small town of St. Joseph.

time of year we are always on the dock or the porch, so it really doesn't matter. But this room allows for excellent "pillow experimentation." Not that I plan it, but every time I have a favorite pair of pillows on my sofa, someone seems to have a pillow emergency and needs them more than I do.

At the end of this room is a big long table with lots of extra leaves. We can get 16 people around that table, but we love to roll it out to the porch when we have 20 or more guests. In the summer, it's common to have maybe eight or ten house guests. Just at cocktail hour, a float boat stops by with ten more people and we are all cajoled into going on a sunset cruise. Next thing you know, it's dark thirty and Michael magically doubles our meal (kind of like the fish and loaves story in the Bible). We roll that table out into the porch and *voila*, dinner for 20. I really don't want to know how he does his magic with the meals. It is truly mindboggling and would cause me stress, but I think it comes from being one of six kids. My forte is rearranging the furniture, squishing more people around the table, and doing the flowers.

You'll notice in the big room that I like to decorate with things that make me smile. If you look at our mantelpiece, which by the way I bought for $35 out of the back of a Ford Pinto—getting it in there should have been worth at least an extra five dollars—but I digress. I love the little French puppets that sometimes perch on the mantel, especially the one with the goofy glasses. And the terra cotta head with the vintage opera costume helmet is my father-in-law's countenance, formed by my husband's little seventh-grade hands. That really makes me smile.

Just off the big room, you can go up the well-worn pickled stairs to a lovely landing that has a great view of the lake. To the right, you'll find the master bedroom with our collection of drawings and prints of Ceres, the goddess of agriculture. I rationalized that each purchase of Ceres would help the cotton harvest or maybe Michael's vegetable garden, but actually I just love the way that the wheat is woven into her hair. The curtains in our bedroom were originally a tablecloth of beautiful soft blue silk with beige French ribbon work. I found it in two pieces at the Paris flea market and immediately envisioned using the fabric to frame the view of the lake from our bedroom.

At the end of the hall opposite our room you'll see my daughter's enormous American Empire bed, which came from Cross Keys plantation. It used to be in our room until we special-ordered a new mattress which surprisingly came in seven inches taller. It is really absurd and we had to give it up years ago when our aging dog could no longer jump that high. Even Michael and I had to get a running start to hurdle into bed. Fortunately our daughter, Sarah Scott, has very long legs. Our guests are usually enchanted by this monstrous piece of family history. We do keep a footstool nearby for the less agile, though we should probably consider a net, since both of our children have battle scars from rolling off at a young age.

Next door is Ross' room. It's smaller than Sarah Scott's because boys don't usually have as much stuff. That's debatable, but now that they are on their own, only occasionally does a baseball glove or prom dress surface, and I am having fun decorating the bedrooms sans athletic stars or Wizard of Oz themes.

Since there is really not enough room for a large bed in Ross' room, the headboard is a Kazak suzani. This is a very special 1930's piece called a Tush Kyiz, which was customarily embroidered by a mother or grandmother for a bride. Traditional weddings and native costumes were suppressed during the Soviet era, so this type of suzani has become rare—and not the kind you can cut up for pillows—or you should be arrested and fined by the Department of Antique Textiles.

The next room along the hallway is the original guest room, and has the only curtains in the house lined with black chintz. We decided that our city friends like the darkness. But if you look out the second floor window, it feels like you are in a secluded treehouse. The colossal live oak's limbs almost touch the window, and Lucille spends torturous hours with her nose to the window being taunted and provoked by the squirrels frolicking in that tree. By the way, did you know those squirrels actually bark at Lucille? It is the damnedest thing.

OPPOSITE A pillow is embellished with ecclesiastic raised-gold metallic embroidery or stumpwork depicting wheat and grapes that symbolize communion in the Christian faith. The Fortuny pillow is a faded silver and pink mid-20th century Persiano pattern. Both pillows are hand trimmed with vintage metallic cording that has been knotted at the corners.

OVERLEAF The wonderful painted wood sculptures of birds are by an unknown west Texas artist. The red cypress barnboards have been distressed with a raw sienna that lightens the color's intensity and gives the room a warm glow year-round. The pink pillow on the French settee has been embellished with raised-gold metallic Ottoman Empire embroidery.

**LEFT** I love the way the bright colors of 20th-century English crewelwork remind me of suzanis from Uzbekistan. For me, this pillow recalls the aesthetics of England's famous Bloomsbury group.

**OPPOSITE** This detail is of a 19th-century suzani I loved but had to pass on as it was in delicate condition and too valuable to cut—and also too expensive!

**OPPOSITE** An unusual antique Swedish secretary with a clock on its side anchors the landing at the top of the stairs. Our daughter Sarah's huge American Empire bed can be glimpsed in the bedroom at the end of the hallway.

**RIGHT** The pillow on a chair in our bedroom was made from a wonderful small 18th-century example of *Or Nue*, or gold shaded embroidery that depicts Our Lady of Sorrows. I decided to make this piece into a pillow for my own collection because I knew I could place it where it would get little use. I found the fragment already framed with its galón. Behind the chair, a 19th-century tablecloth with French ribbon work, has been transformed into curtains.

**OVERLEAF** When I first see a beautiful textile I always look at its reverse. I often find it is as interesting as the front. I also love the way the swirling stitches on the back of this fabric mirror the errant fig ivy vine that sneaked into the breezeway of our house and crept across the tongue and groove.

**PAGES 56–57** I tracked this textile for years in Paris until it finally showed up at a different dealer's booth at a lower price. The 17th-century Italian embroidery was quite damaged and its ground was falling apart. I am now happy that this amazing fragment has a new life.

When I find a wonderful antique textile, I feel a palpable connection to the history of the time of its creation and of the hands that crafted it. I marvel at the dedication and patience involved in creating such intricate and tactile beauty.

**OPPOSITE** Cushions in the Ottoman Empire appear in many artists' renderings throughout the ages, including this colored lithograph of the 1862 *A Turkish Scribe* by American artist Charles Parsons.

**MY LIFE IN STITCHES...**
Seeing all of these pictures
together again reminds me of
all the fun and the adventures
my family and I have had while
searching for wonderful fabrics.

# Getting down to business

Let's go back downstairs, taking time to get a whiff of the rosemary chicken Michael is grilling, and back through the breezeway to the studio: The International Headquarters of B.Viz Design. Seriously, I can get pillows from St. Joseph, Louisiana, to Abu Dhabi in 36 hours.

I love walking into the studio with the glimmer of silver and gold embroideries peeking out from antique textiles stacked to the ceiling. (It's probably an OCD person's greatest nightmare.) But the colors, textures, and patinas still make my pulse quicken. Like the sparkle of sunlight or moonlight on the lake, there is something magical about a little shimmer.

Basically, I work at a table in the middle of the studio, with surrounding shelves of categorized textile fragments. They range from 17th- and 18th-century tapestries to 20th-century suzanis, from 18th- and 19th-century toiles to 19th- and 20th-century raised-metallic embroidery. And I love my mounds of lusciously hued Fortuny fabrics. I can almost reach each piece I want to work with and I have to actually see everything in order to pull together the perfect elements and patinas. This can be a very disorderly endeavor. When I do manage to get it all cleaned up and extremely organized, I find I become paralyzed because I don't want to mess it all up again. But if everything is too disheveled, I don't have space to design. For me there is a fine line of organized chaos that I seem to have to achieve before I can be in my most creative mode.

In this present-day society, time is such a precious commodity. Since I have been making pillows from antique textile fragments for over 20 years, I've developed a special relationship with time. I marvel at the amount of time that was originally expended constructing so many of these treasured works. And I am proud of the countless hours we spend bringing many of these almost-lost textiles back to life.

An interesting part of my story is that I do this from a tiny remote place where I can't even buy thread. While originally I thought this was a disadvantage, I now credit the contrast of my city and country experiences for helping to sharpen my vision. Keeping one foot in the rural North Louisiana Delta, and one foot in the high-end design world makes each environment feel more stimulating. I find the energy of the city and the events of the art and design industry motivational and exciting. Returning to this special haven of nature on the banks of Lake Bruin, I see my natural environment more keenly and discover the colors and textures around me surfacing in my pillow designs.

This book is a visual feast if you like textiles, design, and nature. I've tried to explain the nuances of my work and to develop an appreciation for the true craftsmanship of our studio and the almost-extinct needle talent of so long ago. The textiles that I use for my pillows are not the kind that are exhibited in museums or collected by professional experts, but pieces that I see repeatedly in my travels, and I try to give them a new life. I am very conscious of the fine line between destroying a textile and saving a valuable piece of beauty exemplifying the love, devotion, and time that went into creating it.

But let me back up and tell you how the studio came about. It all began with a rather ridiculous period in my life that ended up being quite pivotal. After our daughter was born in the mid-1980s, I wanted to stay home with her, but we were young, newly married, and needed two incomes. Spending $75 on baby booties, little sneakers, tiny T-shirts, and fabric paint, I then embellished these plain white surfaces with rosebuds, polka dots, bows, zigzags, and splatter paint. Aptly displaying them in a basket with a bow, I sold the whole collection, basket and all, to an upscale children's clothing store. Then I did it again with a bigger basket. I called my college roommate and fellow art major, who had been successfully hand-painting T-shirts since the New Orleans World Fair. Amy immediately invited me to join her booth at the Dallas Trade Mart. To my amazement, I left that show with a gazillion orders, and sage business advice from Amy: "Keep taking orders! You'll figure out how to fill them." Not only was I overwhelmed; I didn't have enough money to buy that much inventory.

OPPOSITE When I'm at a flea market, I can't help trying on an outfit or two. By completely immersing myself in beautiful textiles, the rich history becomes overwhelmingly palpable. Besides, I love a great jacket.

OVERLEAF LEFT An 18th-century hand-woven tapestry fragment, ready for some repair work, appears to depict daffodils, and makes me think of the origins of the plants it portrays, and how long things we commonly see today have actually existed in the past.

OVERLEAF RIGHT This colorful collection of tiny tapestry fragments will eventually be made into petite pillows.

A dread came over me, realizing that I was going to have to apply for a loan. I didn't really think it was going to be a problem, since my dad was the president of the local bank, but I knew it was not going to be fun. He is a natural-born devil's advocate, and I was going to have to stay on my toes. After compiling a very meticulous spreadsheet of all the numbers, fluffing up the impressive stack of orders (just for show), and harnessing all my 27 years of lifetime experience, he turned me down.

I left the bank fighting back tears (because crying was not going to look professional) and feeling a fierce determination unlike anything I'd ever felt before.

I called each customer (remember, this was before the internet) and asked if the terms could be changed to C.O.D., to generate faster cash flow. Everyone agreed, and like at the start of a race, paint started flying, baby clothes and cash cycled in and out so fast I was dizzy. Having a newborn probably didn't help, but fortunately she was an angel. (It's actually difficult to remember the details because it was all one big colorful blur.)

After working myself to death, and plowing all the profits back into more inventory for the growing business, I decided to approach my sock supplier at the time with an idea. What if I just painted the socks for McCubbin Hosiery? We would be able to give the customer the same product for a better price. I would not have to buy the inventory and would charge per dozen, depending on the difficulty of the design. Within a few months they had sold my splatter-painted designs to JC Penney, and 18 wheelers started arriving at my house. We would lay the socks in the yard and sling paint like Jackson Pollock. We could do 200 dozen a day—and I became better at forecasting the weather than any TV station. Soon, other large stores bought the socks. As I said, it was a ridiculous way to make money, but it really worked. At one time, I had 26 people in this small town of 1100 working, and we were all benefiting.

Soon, I decorated our house with the windfall, then friends from New Orleans wanted my help, and next came friends of friends. I had accidentally become an interior designer, and somehow was now working all over the country.

I was always frustrated with how much time, energy, and expense went into making pillows just out of nice fabric from a design center. It seemed like the pillow design always took longer to determine than the sofas or drapery. During one of my early projects in New York, I wanted a touch of age for a modern chair. I was thrilled to be in Manhattan, thinking I was going to find the perfect pillow source. Every antique textile pillow I found was overflowing with passementerie and, well, was just too frou-frou. I wanted something with clean lines. So after trudging countless miles around the city looking for pillows, I finally ended up at the 26th Street flea market. I found a lovely pair of 19th-century curtain panels with a simple gold filigree border. In another booth, I found a tattered religious vestment with its gold metallic ribbon the only part that could be salvaged—and it had the perfect patina. The first pillow was created in my mind, standing right there on the pavement at 26th and Sixth Avenue.

After completing my client's pillow, I had enough of the fabulous curtain fabric to make a few more pillows. I took them to Gerrie Bremermann, a design legend in New Orleans who had a fantastic store fronting her interior design business. She loved them, sold them quickly, and wanted more. Fortunately, I was still visiting New York regularly and working on a country home in Connecticut. I frequented the same flea market and also found more textiles on Magazine Street in New Orleans. Soon I began looking for antique textiles and trims wherever I went, and for three years sold my pillows only to my clients and Bremermann Designs.

After I gradually accumulated a nice bevy of pillows, I tried another trade show to see if I could grow the pillow part of my business. Just as I was about to leave, after three days with no sales, one of the former editors of *Veranda* magazine purchased two pillows, gushing the whole time about how much she loved them, and how well they were priced for the quality of the craftsmanship. That certainly boosted my spirits. Then,

lo and behold, a buyer from Neiman Marcus discovered me, and ordered the pillows for 22 of their stores. Instantly, I had outgrown the 26th Street flea market and was bound for Paris.

Let me back up again and tell you why this was such a life-saving development. I have to admit that I love cities. I had this crazy, beautiful mother who loved to travel and dragged me all over creation. I think coming from such a small place, where generations of my family had lived, I was always wide-eyed to the world. Everywhere else was so different and, to tell you the truth, I took my rural surroundings for granted. My mother and her exciting travels definitely planted the seeds of my wanderlust. After graduating from Newcomb College at Tulane University, I thought I would get a little experience in my beloved New Orleans before moving to New York, or Europe, or anywhere exciting, for that matter. Out of nowhere, my knight in shining armor, an adorable Uptown New Orleans boy with the biggest, most infectious smile, materialized in my life, and my plans were thwarted. Next thing I knew, I was an art teacher in Shreveport, Louisiana, and soon discovered I was having a baby. (Consequently, painting baby clothes started there.) After a serious bout of professional pouting, I persuaded my husband to move back to New Orleans. Just as I thought my life was getting back on track, my father convinced my husband and me that he needed help with the small-town community bank that was growing (which had, by the way, originally denied my loan). To my horror, as hard as I had worked to escape this really rural country life, I was back in the thick of it, paintbrush in hand, infant on one hip, and another baby on the way.

The upside of this predicament was that my daughter was thrilled to be the only grandchild and dubbed her grandfather Touchdown, which I probably don't have to explain. My husband absolutely loved the agrarian lifestyle and proved to be an excellent banker. A wonderful lady named Belinda arrived on the scene to help my domestic situation with Sarah (and the soon-to-arrive Ross), and the industrious Belinda also helped me with the sock-painting enterprise. We were building our house on Lake Bruin, and luckily had lots of grass for splattering socks.

After getting a bit of age on Ross, making money with the socks, and getting requests for decorating in New Orleans, Michael encouraged me to take a stab at interior design. Further spurring this change was the fact that my expert pouting technique to get out of town was no longer effective, which was good, because I was getting tired of myself. I loved dashing off to the big metropolis to see what was new, and to watch creative projects come together. Then I would happily return home for the kids' homework, school and athletic events, or playtime on the lake. The contrast of this 'dual citizenship' of country and city life eventually created a tremendous appreciation for both worlds. To have Michael and the kids meet me somewhere new at the end of a workweek and watch them soaking up different cultures was very gratifying. Ross was particularly fascinated by cab drivers with turbans. And Sarah was impressed with my speed at catching the cabs. At a very young age, she pointed out that I never moved that fast at home.

I started trying to figure out a way to slow down the decorating and build up the pillow business. (Because let me tell you, contrary to popular belief, interior designers have very stressful jobs.) The Neiman Marcus order and the trip to France had helped tremendously and, most of all, beefed up my inventory of antique textiles. As my pillows started showing up in national magazines, *Southern Accents* did a whole page on my business in 2002. I scrambled to find someone to build a website. It was up and running just before the article was published and it was life-altering. Suddenly I didn't have to drive around selling pillows from the trunk of my car (a literal trunk show), but could show the world what I had created over the Internet. It was like magic, and the pillow side of my business boomed.

I have been traveling to France once a year since the Neiman Marcus order, but after the increasing business on the website (and my perpetual wanderlust), I started adding other destinations to my circuit, such as Holland, Belgium, Italy, Spain, Argentina, Peru, Turkey, and Africa. The good thing about textiles is they are everywhere. And you learn a lot about a culture from its textiles. Of course, Michael likes Italy the best, due to the cuisine.

**OPPOSITE** This frame contains more pieces of exquisite embroidery in many shades of gold from Europe and Turkey. When designing a pillow with this type of work, I often rearrange the designs to come up with a more pleasing and original composition.

**OVERLEAF** Bulletin boards covered in linen display many of the antique textile components that have been saved. Besides keeping the pieces safe, the boards help my design process as I can readily see what is available to be used.

When he joins me not only do we hunt for antique textiles, but we also check out grocery stores wherever we go. In Istanbul, my favorite city, we walked into a big grocery store in search of uncommon ingredients and to my delight found a Turkish *House Beautiful,* with one of my pillows on the cover. And Michael found a hot sauce he had never seen. It was a banner day!

I find it hard to explain when people ask where I find my antique textiles. If you have a passion for something, you look for it wherever you go. When you do this all the time, I think you develop a sixth sense or some kind of intuitive radar. One of my best scores was in Comfort, Texas, of all places, when I was on my way to pick up my daughter at summer camp. A friend told me it was a cute town so I pulled off the interstate to do a drive-by. I noticed a charming little antique store and discovered that the owners had bought an armoire from Mexico that, unbeknownst to them, was full of old, worn-out vestments. They had almost thrown them away.

The metallic ribbon (galón or galloon) that I so often use is difficult to find, especially one with a good patina. You just can't imagine the deconstructing that goes on at the studio, or on the road, for that matter. I have spent many hours the last night of a trip at an outdoor café, dismantling textiles so I can lighten the load for shipping and carrying them home. The best purchase that helped accelerate my design process was a big trunk full of different shades, sizes, and lengths of antique metallic galón. It took every ounce of self-control to bargain for that trunk. And I got my price because I told the dealer I would give him a fair price if he measured each piece in the trunk, one-by-one. And I knew that was the last thing he wanted to do. Score B.Viz!

What people don't realize is that I might spend an hour digging through my treasure trove of galón to find one with the perfect patina. Just as I am satisfied I have found the precise coloration, I will measure the piece and discover the galón is an inch too short. I am such a dysfunctional perfectionist I won't jeopardize the composition of the design, so I will either keep looking through my stash, or shelve that design until I find the perfect trim on my next trip. See why I had to give up interior design? My clients were all happy with my work, but it drove me crazy trying to get a project to my ideal. I can get a pillow to be perfect and that says a lot about my wonderfully talented seamstresses.

Belinda (yes, my former housekeeper and nanny) is now my web master, bookkeeper, right arm, and part-time seamstress. She knows me like the back of her hand, and does all she can in her power to keep me focused. When I turn around at the end of our gravel road to retrieve whatever I just realized I forgot, she walks out of the door and hands it to me before I even ask for it. I am convinced she is psychic, but, more important, she is so very patient and kind. And I do like that she can read my mind.

Monica is a miracle. She arrived in our quaint village after evacuating from Hurricane Katrina and has become a permanent citizen along with her husband and dog. (Population now 1103, counting the dog.) She is incredibly talented and patient. Respecting each special textile, she never cuts corners. Unlike me, she is very focused and a functional perfectionist. What really amazes me about Monica is that I will bring her the most daunting project and she doesn't flinch. Her repair work on the metallic embroideries matches the original technique, and she uses antique metallic threads of different patinas to make the repairs. She sews in a very academic manner.

Brenda is also a functional perfectionist and has the incredible patience to repair tapestries. But my favorite moment with Brenda was when she hopped out of her car to drop off pillows for no more than 45 seconds. She came running back shrieking that her car had been stolen. It was very surreal because that just doesn't happen around here. I grabbed the phone to call 911 and we started running down the gravel road looking for the culprits. That year we had corn planted in the big field in front of our house and it was probably eight feet high. As we ran farther down the road with 911 on the phone, we noticed an odd pattern in the cornfield. Unbeknownst to Brenda, she had inadvertently left the car in reverse, and while she was in the studio it had stealthily crept backwards. The car had mowed down a path through the cornfield, coming to a halt against a massive pile of cornstalks. It was corn-jacked. As you can see, we have a lot of excitement out here in the country.

**OPPOSITE** The rolls of recycled galóns, or metallic ribbons, display the subtlety of the patinas I use when creating a pillow composition.

**OVERLEAF LEFT** I sketch each of the designs of my pillows on a two-part sheet, so my seamstress can get one with the instructions and measurements and I keep the other for my records. The negative space is just as important to my design process as the works of art. Each pillow ends up being a big mathematical equation when I decipher the price of everything by the inch.

**OVERLEAF RIGHT** The antique elements are mocked up and measured precisely during the design process.

Speaking of excitement, I have to tell you about Marina. I noticed Marina Tosini one early morning at the Porte de Vanves outdoor market in Paris. She was meandering through the booths and reminded me of a European version of my sweet Southern Belle grandmother. After a bit, I ran into her at a textile booth and she heard me trying to communicate that I just wanted to buy the trim and not the whole textile. My French is a horrible combination of Cajun French with a Southern drawl, which makes it pretty much frightening to any nationality. Marina turned to me and said in a perfect Mrs. Doubtfire accent, "May I be of assistance?" Within a minute she had negotiated a fabulous price that I would never have gotten for the precious galón. She asked what I did, and was impressed with the photographs of my pillows. We walked farther down the street, and I could tell she was summing me up, scrutinizing what I found interesting. Finally, when I passed her inspection, she invited me to go with her to the Foire de Chatou. After a delightful, rewarding day at the Chatou market, we went back to her cottage for tea and a tour of her most impressive antiques collection. My heart swelled as I felt as if I had been gifted another day with my grandmother. Marina was 79 at the time.

She quickly became a buyer for me, also my antique textile mentor, and actually my life mentor. Her wonderfully positive attitude is completely contagious. I am sure it is the reason for her longevity. She is 95 now and still busily working though has recently stopped driving. After our first encounter when she was 79, I went back to France and stayed with her for a week. I discovered she is not a sweet, docile old lady, but a fiery Italian who drives like a bat out of hell. I had met my partner in crime, and oh, have we had some adventures! She is one of the best bargainers I know, because she gets away with that sweet little old lady act. After she does something that leaves me speechless she will often turn to me and say, "You know I am a Leo." Then she roars like a lion. And this is usually while she is driving 120 kilometers an hour and shaking her fist out the window at someone who cut her off.

Her gracious and jovial niece, Cinzia, originally from Padua, makes the best foie gras I have ever tasted, and serves some of the most delicious meals in France. Ludwig, her German husband, is a master ébéniste and the calm one of the bunch. A mishmash of French, Italian, German, and English shoots around the table like a pinball machine. I usually pick up a new expression or two and they all laugh hysterically at my pronunciation, especially after a few glasses of wine.

I have to say, as much as I love making beautiful things, it's a bigger story than that. The wonderful people I've met along the way, and the incredible talent that was hidden in this tiny town is the real tale. I feel as if I have come full circle from trying to escape the cards that life dealt me, to playing each one with gratitude. I was previously motivated by the next trip, but now I'm motivated by seeing people prosper in our economically disparate area. The challenge of doing business from home makes the victories even sweeter. On top of all this, I get to make beautiful things. That's what we, in Louisiana, call lagniappe—a little something extra. I feel very lucky to have crossed paths and worked with such wonderful and interesting people, and to have my job take me off the beaten path (even though I live off the beaten path).

I am currently sitting on my dock writing and thinking as I stare at the glistening water on this beautiful spring day. It has just dawned on me that life is like the Mississippi River. It twists and churns, swirls, and sometimes gets big, full, and angry. It changes course and wreaks havoc and anxiety, and then it calms down and once again becomes the peaceful meandering giant that lulls us all along. This happens despite the levees meant to control and guide it.

Much like Mother Nature and my gardener, neither the river nor life are entirely subject to our control. Yet here is the beautiful thing about this: The river's sinuous changes and seasonal rebellions are responsible for depositing the layers of treasures that make up our rich alluvial soil. And life's unplanned twists and shifts bathe us with memories and experiences far greater and more meaningful than what we could have planned. These struggles are responsible for the rich patina of our souls.

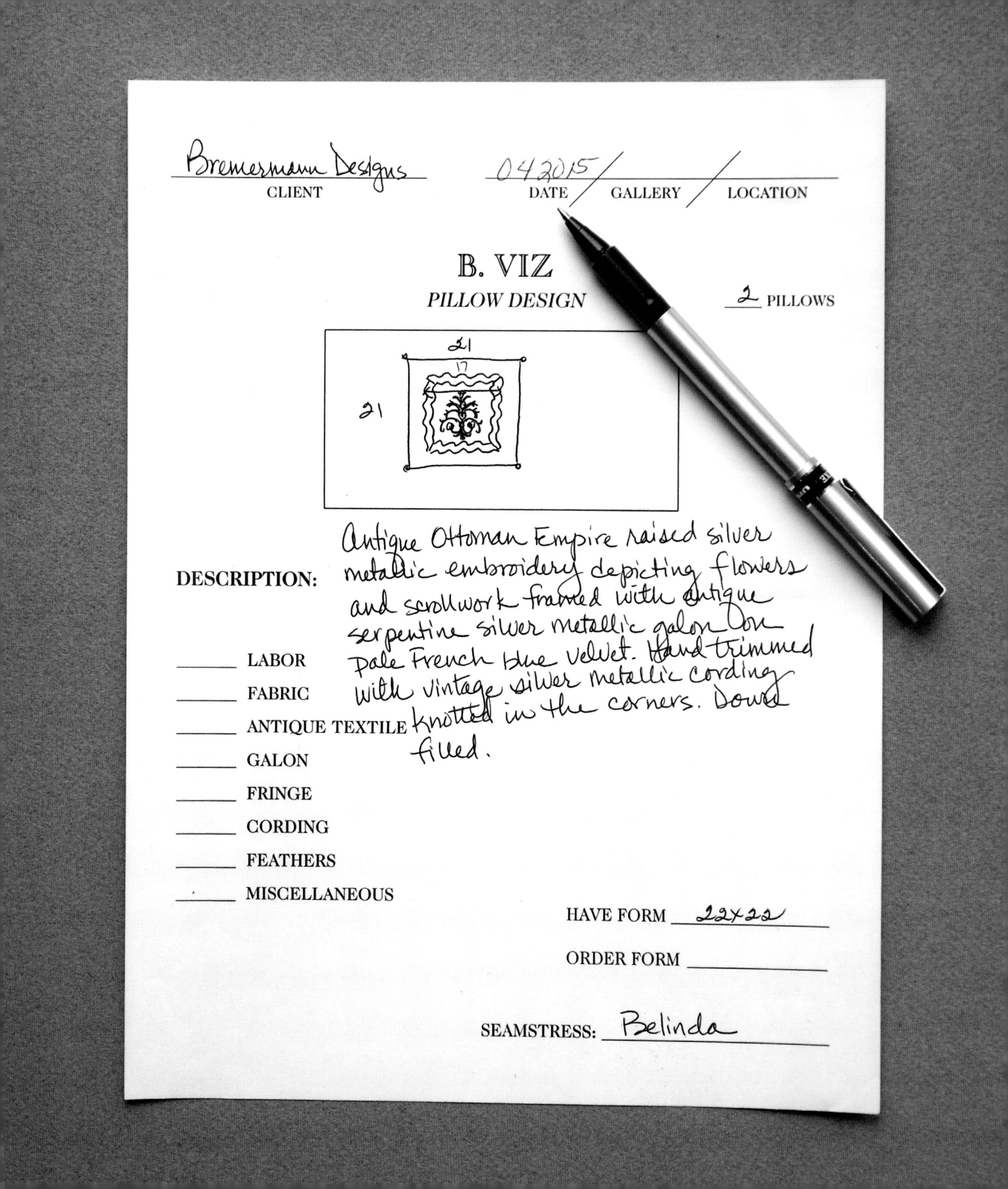

Bremermann Designs
CLIENT

042015 / / 
DATE / GALLERY / LOCATION

# B. VIZ
*PILLOW DESIGN*

<u>2</u> PILLOWS

**DESCRIPTION:**

Antique Ottoman Empire raised silver metallic embroidery depicting flowers and scrollwork framed with antique serpentine silver metallic galon on pale French blue velvet. Hand trimmed with vintage silver metallic cording knotted in the corners. Down filled.

_____ LABOR

_____ FABRIC

_____ ANTIQUE TEXTILE

_____ GALON

_____ FRINGE

_____ CORDING

_____ FEATHERS

_____ MISCELLANEOUS

HAVE FORM ___22x22___

ORDER FORM _____

SEAMSTRESS: ___Belinda___

Be sure to miter the corners of the antique silver metallic serpentine gallon.

Line up flowers and all branches for scrollwork and leaves to be symmetrical.

Use the lighter nap of the the velvet to get more of a contrast with the silver color of the textile.

Repair broken antique raised Ottoman embroidery with old silver metallic threads of the same patina. Use dival stitch technique.

**PREVIOUS PAGES** Monica, *left,* Belinda, *right,* and I get together in the attic workspace of my studio. Monica is reapplying aged gold appliqués in a more modern pattern. Belinda is salvaging the embroidery from a vestment fragment.

**RIGHT** Monica meticulously reapplies the padded *dival* embroidery salvaged from a late 19th-century Turkish *bindalli,* or kaftan-type garment, to a hardier velvet ground. After measuring the spacing precisely. she tacks it down, and then goes back around the perimeter of the design with tiny, invisible stitches, *left.* When designing a pillow such as this 18th-century verdure tapestry fragment, I pin where the textile will meet the seam, then place the trim in the best position for a pleasing composition. After I'm satisfied that the scale is correct, I draw the pillow's image on a two-part design sheet with measurements to $\frac{1}{16}$ th of an inch. I then figure the cost of all materials by the square inch, write a description of the pillow and its heritage, and make notes to the seamstresses, *center.* Belinda works on a 19th-century ecclesiastical fragment I found in Paris. With nerves of steel, she carefully removes the vining raised-gold metallic embroidery with sharp cuticle scissors. One slip and the precious embroidery could unravel, *right.*

Learning about textiles is a bit like taking a history class. Throughout the ages, every culture has created its own versions of patterns and weavings. These are some of my favorites.

OPPOSITE Paintings from the past —as in John de Critz the Elder's 1605 portrait of Anne of Denmark, have taught me a great deal about textile and fashion history. Sometimes it is difficult to date textiles because many fabric and trim designs have been copied throughout the ages. Today, fabric houses often have historic collections and recreate many patterns from the past.

# TEXTILE CATEGORY: SUZANI

The first suzani I ever bought was in Paris, long before these bold, colorful Uzbek embroidered textiles started gracing the pages of magazines and flooding the market. I paid a fortune for it, but luckily it was a rare 19th century example. I was completely floored by the sheer number of hand stitches, and the intricate patterns and colors just dazzled me. The piece was too good to cut, and went straight into my personal collection.

Suzani means "needle" in Persian and suzanis were originally made in Uzbekistan and other central Asian countries. With a daughter's birth, the tradition of family and friends embroidering suzanis for her dowry begins. Narrow widths of fabric, usually cotton or silk, or a combination of cotton and silk, are loosely stitched together so the artist can draw the design. Then the strips were divided amongst the seamstresses and individually embroidered. After each was completed, they were sewn back together. Often the stitches did not match perfectly at the seam or the dye lots for the threads were slightly off. These imperfections make me smile and think of the hands—from grandmother to child—who played a part in the existence of each suzani.

There are many factors involved when I work with suzanis. An old, hand-stitched suzani in good condition should never be cut. Often I find fragments that are old, torn suzanis and try to salvage what I can to make pillows. Many need to be backed for durability. They often have little blemishes because they were actually used as wall hangings, draperies, bedspreads, personal attire, decorations for weddings, and protective coverings. Many times a gorgeous piece I want to work with will include a color I think is hideous and I know will not sell. It makes finding old fragments difficult for the decorating market. There also are many new hand- and machine-stitched suzanis that are quite beautiful, and have more pleasing colors. And it is wonderful to see this tradition of embroidery continuing in Central Asia. For me, finding an old suzani with pleasing colors and in good condition is a wonderful triumph.

Along with their popularity, more is now being written about suzanis and the culture of their region. Twenty years ago, all I knew was that I loved the spirit of their color and the energy of their thousands of hand stitches. Now I can't read enough about this Central Asian culture and their crafts, particularly the showstopper suzanis.

**ABOVE** In 1906, the Belle of Tashkent, in a wedding costume of Russian printed cotton, poses in front of a locally hand-stitched suzani.

**OPPOSITE** The quirkiness of the design in this beautifully colored scrap of a 20th-century chain-stitched suzani is a clue to its hand craftsmanship.

**OVERLEAF** A rare early-20th century Kazakh Tus-Kiiz that is too special to cut makes a wonderful headboard in my son's old room. The intricate hand-embroidered chain-stitched tent hanging could have been sewn by a grandmother or handed down from a mother to her daughter. These especially revered suzanis were used at weddings and then hung in a place of prominence in the newlyweds' home. The bottom of this Mongolian- and Chinese-influenced design was left unfinished as a custom to make sure the marriage would flourish and bring joy to the couple.

**OPPOSITE** The "flowering bush" suzani motif in shades of cream and berry, with a chocolate outline, makes festive pillows for the always-lively screened porch. This design is typically from the Samarkand area of Uzbekistan, though I found the modern suzani in Istanbul.

**RIGHT 1.** A pillow created from a hand-stitched 20th-century Samarkand suzani depicts the "flowering bush" motif. It is not surprising that these expressive designs have been compared to French artist Henry Matisse's cut-out paper works. **2.** Unusual soft pinks and creams adorn this beautiful 20th-century Uzbek suzani I found in Marrakesh. While I was not particularly looking for Central Asian pieces in Morocco, I couldn't pass up the exceptional colors and knew it would make gorgeous pillows. **3.** This sunny pillow is from the same suzani as the one on the screened porch. The flowering bushes were in alternating colors on the large embroidery so I was able to get several pairs of each colorway in yellow, berry, cream, and chocolate. **4.** I love the patterns of the finely worked cotton chain stitches on this Kazakhstan suzani pillow. Many of these types of suzanis come from an area near the border of Kazakhstan, Russia, and China. Mongolian and Chinese influences are apparent in the meticulous ornamentation. **5.** A newer hand-embroidered suzani is believed to be from the culturally traditional southernmost areas of Uzbekistan. This pillow has the native characteristics of cheerful floral medallions often stitched on red cotton grounds and made for wedding decorations. **6.** Grey was not a typical color for suzanis, so it is possible that the ground for this flowering bush Samarkand suzani was originally blue, and has faded to this grey patina. **7.** This mid-20th century embroidered suzani pillow from Tajikistan has the typical bold flat patterns on a black ground. These suzanis were usually made in limited colors, and this one is probably quite faded from age. **8.** A new suzani that I found at a show in the United States intrigued me with its unusual colors. I loved the bold aqua and pink couched satin stitches with the strong black vines and other bright colors outlined in white. I can't determine the origin of the design but am delighted to know that there is a market for this traditionally important Central Asian craft to flourish.

# TEXTILE CATEGORY: ECCLESIASTICAL

Ecclesiastical or religious needlework provides a rich history of European embroidery styles and techniques. The combination of faith, money, and power was responsible for some of the most labor intensive and glorious displays of embroidery art in the name of the church. My favorite museum pieces to examine are from the Middle Ages through the 17th century and are Biblical figurative designs on religious textiles such as vestments and altar frontals. The expressive faces of these renowned holy people look like they've been painted with thread using a detailed split stitch. A technique called *Or Nue* (or shaded gold) was used to give their garments a three-dimensional quality and reflect light. The best examples can be found in museums and private collections. Finding a textile of this age in exemplary condition is rare.

Most of the metallic embroidered pieces I use from tattered vestments and banners are from the 19th and 20th centuries. Embroidery was cultivated in the convents as well as in some monasteries. Ladies of noble households were also extremely talented with the needle and there have been records showing that many donated embroidery to the church as well. The tightly and meticulously raised metallic embroidered designs are often stitched over cardboard, thickly cut paper, felt, or leather, and sometimes even wood. It is fascinating to deconstruct the components of these textiles and discover their backings. Sometimes I'll find that the design was drawn on old newsprint, book or Bible pages, or ledgers with beautiful calligraphy. The metallic stitches are so perfect you can only see the human touch by looking at the backs of these creations. I love to save the beautiful gold work on distressed grounds by carefully detaching it and reapplying the pieces by hand to sturdier fabrics like velvet or linen. Also, the worn threads can be restored with our numerous spools and range of patinas from antique metallic threads. I always save the metallic ribbon to frame or border my pillow designs. The vestment backing and the handspun linen from the lining are used for the miniature Christmas-stocking ornaments we create from all the scraps.

Recycling is not new to the ecclesiastical world. Vestments have always been made with some of the most glorious fabrics. In the past, aristocratic families were known to donate their unwanted clothing to the church. The dresses were disassembled and reworked into magnificent liturgical pieces. Also, ecclesiastical styles changed over the ages, and many times, older vestments were remade to suit more contemporary church fashions.

With the rise of many inactive churches in rural Europe and with the declining number of members in the churches, many are being deconsecrated, and their treasures should be handled with only the utmost reverence.

**ABOVE** The emperor Charlemagne wears a long, embroidered stole and glorious ornate cope in this vintage engraving. This portrait in grand ecclesiastical finery is from the *Magasin Pittoresque*, Paris, 1843.

**OPPOSITE** An antique religious vestment depicting the Lamb of God needs minor repair work on the front.

**OVERLEAF** A dilapidated 18th-century chasuble with fairly good gold work shows how the patina has, over time, darkened in areas. I would love to remake this for a priest who appreciates its antiquity. Because the metallic embroidery is very heavy, he would need to be in prime physical condition to wear the garment.

**OPPOSITE** This outstanding and unusually large 19th-century appliqué, removed from a damaged European altar frontal, and sent by one of my vendors in France, depicts a pelican feeding her young with her own blood. It is the perfect analogy in the Christian church to Christ giving his blood to save the souls of the faithful.

**RIGHT 1.** I believe that this thickly raised gold-metallic embroidery of flora came from a Belgian convent. The high-relief work is over carved wood forms. This type of decoration is more difficult to find and more challenging to repair because the surfaces are not flat. **2.** This lily appliqué of cloth of gold was splattered with white chalky plaster in a box of similar textiles at Paris' Porte de Vanves antiques market. I picked the crusty layer off the appliqués, vacuumed them, and discovered they were each backed with the most beautiful sepia calligraphy. **3.** When damaged silk embroidery from the center area of the classic and timeless quatrefoil was removed, it left a clean-lined design that is one of my favorites. Removed from a worn-out vestment, the four lobes of the quatrefoil symbolize the evangelists Matthew, Mark, Luke, and John. **4.** It is hard to believe this modern looking design was removed from an early 20th-century vestment I found in Rouen, France. In the center of the raised silver-metallic embroidered eight-pointed star was the Christogram, IHS, the monogram of the Greek name for Jesus Christ. **5.** I like to look for components I can rearrange like the raised-silver metallic branches from an early-20th-century altar frontal. Parts of the antique textile were beyond repair, but the branches were in perfect condition, so I placed them to look like a neo-classical wreath. **6.** The wheat and grapes of this high-relief gold-metallic embroidery are also from an altar frontal, and represent the Holy Eucharist—wheat for the body of Christ and wine for the blood of Christ. **7.** I found a scrap of silk embellished with this fantastic embroidered appliqué of a bow with arrows in a quiver, probably from a church banner in honor of St. Sebastian. **8.** This beautiful 19th-century metallic embroidered appliqué of a pelican was sent to me by one of my vendors in France. The pelican is the state bird of Louisiana and I incorporated this emblem in a pillow for the governor's mansion, early in my career.

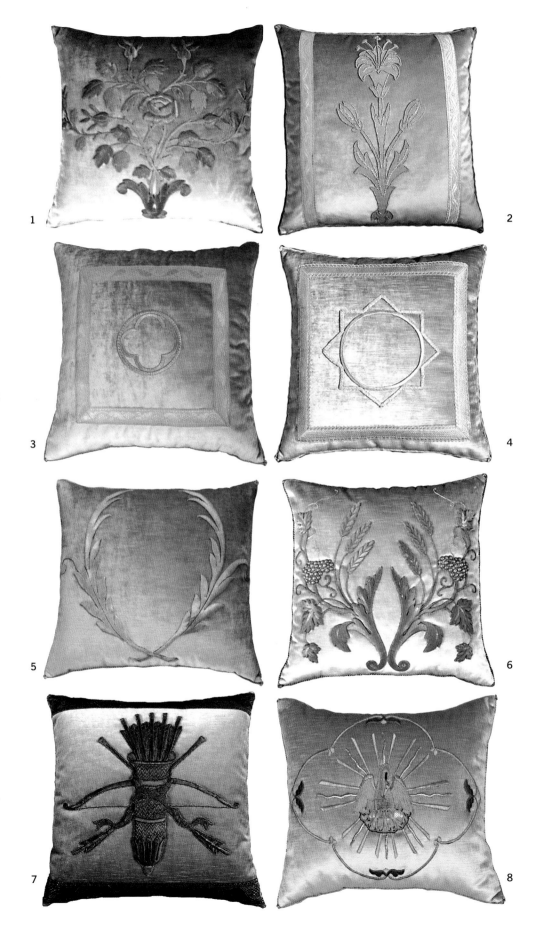

# TEXTILE CATEGORY: FORTUNY

Oddly enough, I seem to have always known about Fortuny fabric. As a young child, I once identified a Fortuny fabric, much to my mother's and her friend's amazement. On my first trip to Venice, I had a *déjà vu* moment with my friends when I envisioned and predicted the building we would see around the next corner. So it's no surprise how much I love Fortuny textiles. I'm drawn to their watery complexion—so Venetian—and the depth of the magical prints on Fortuny's crunchy Egyptian cotton. (Though I would prefer it to be the cotton from my front yard!)

At first I used only old Fortuny remnants for my pillows, but once the demand grew, I started collecting any scraps of Fortuny I could find—especially those with a nice patina. It seemed as if a piece that was even a few years old had started to mellow and take on a personality of its own. Truly, the gold- and silver-metallic pigment starts out much shinier, and slowly melds into a lovely patina.

Mariano Fortuny was an absolute genius. His inventions in indirect lighting techniques revolutionized the theater in the early 20th century. Being an artist and photographer as well, he saw the stage as a three-dimensional painting in motion. Around 1909, he fabricated the finely accordion-pleated Delphos gown, which was inspired by classical Greek sculptures and clung to the body, unlike the fashions of the time. Designed to be worn with only minimal undergarments, only the most daring ladies, like the dancer Isadora Duncan, wore the silk concoctions. But by the 1920s, Fortuny's pleated dresses were becoming acceptable for wearing in public. He also created his own dyes for these dresses and his soon-to-become legendary line of home-decorating textiles. The many designs he devised for his interior fabrics range in influence from the Italian Renaissance to tribal patterns. His brilliance is evident, because these designs are still as much in vogue today as they were when he first introduced them. Fortuny fabric is what you get when you combine a creative inventor with a chemist, an artist, a historian, a traveler, and with a large dose of genius.

**ABOVE** The legendary Mariano Fortuny (1871-1949) blended his genius in art, science, and technology to have an eternal influence on the world of fashion, interior design, and theater.

**OPPOSITE** A very early Peruviano Fortuny fabric with the Società Anonima Fortuny stamp was found by Marina Tosini, my dear 95-year-old Italian friend and textile expert. This marking was used beginning in 1919, when Fortuny and his partner, Giancarlo Stucky, began creating printed fabrics at its factory in the Giudecca area in Venice, Italy.

**OVERLEAF** In the breezeway of our house, the colors of old and new Fortuny fabrics feel almost ethereal. The subtlety of the glazes on the local clay of the McCarty pottery from Merigold, Mississippi, has a similar effect. The dripping dark-brown glaze squiggle on the pitchers signifies the Mississippi River.

SOC. AN. FORTVNV

**OPPOSITE** This very old, sumptuous Fortuny pattern was hand-printed in a lush blue with a hint of green and natural, almost homespun-looking ground. The areas of rich blue are darker or lighter depending on the pressure of the hand that printed it. This fragment came from a drapery panel and the vendor told me it was from the 1920s.

**RIGHT 1.** A Melagrana Fortuny pillow in marmalade and silvery gold is hand-trimmed with a tiny vintage silver metallic-military cording knotted in the corners. The Melagrana pattern is a repeating pomegranate form that is often seen in Persian artwork. **2.** A very old Granada Fortuny pillow is thought to be from the 1940s. The dark blue-green and gold design is a Spanish pattern named for the city of Mariano Fortuny's birth. **3.** Campanelle Fortuny is an Italian design from the 17th century, with a morning glory theme. This beautiful blue-green and silvery gold Campanelle pillow is finished with our signature hand-trimmed tiny vintage cording with knotted corners. **4.** This rich royal purple and silvery gold pillow is in a current Carnavalet color and pattern. A 17th-century French design, it is named for the Parisian museum. In 1926, Elsie McNeill Lee first discovered Fortuny fabrics in the Carnavalet Museum, and introduced the work to the United States, carrying the business forward after Fortuny's death. **5.** The 16th century Italian painter Veronese inspired the name of this Fortuny pattern. This pillow is in a warm French brown and gold, finished with the tiny, vintage gold-metallic cording that was often originally used for military uniforms. **6.** A vintage Orsini Fortuny pillow in off-white and silvery gold was once a drapery panel. The Orsini pattern is an Italian 17th-century design named for the powerful Orsini family of Medieval and Renaissance Rome. **7.** Dandolo Fortuny is named after the famous Venetian family, and the pattern was born from a 17th century Italian design. This pillow is in a vintage, no-longer-available color, in a soft raspberry red and mellow gold. **8.** The Moresco Fortuny pillow in bittersweet and warm white is a currently available fabric. The pattern is based on an early Moorish design. I marvel at its contemporary flavor although it has been around for so many years. I opted not to trim this pillow, so as to play up its clean lines and modern feel.

# TEXTILE CATEGORY: EUROPEAN EMBROIDERY

I have grouped these fabrics together under European Embroidery because there are so many embroidery types from the different countries. Styles range from primitive monograms to elaborate goldwork embroidery. The scope of embroidery techniques and abilities is immense. Some of the fragments I have discovered were probably made domestically, yet others could have been made by an embroidery guild. Some of the guilds were so strict and professional that the sewing could only be done during daylight hours: The lack of light affected the quality of the embroidery. Just think about how much of this work was created before electricity! I love to find curtains with embroidered borders to make long pillows. I sometimes unearth hand-worked pillow fronts that need some tender loving care. Panels from bedding and table runners are also sources for some of my pillows.

One of my most favorite pieces I ever bought was part of a crazy quilt made in 19th century France from mostly 18th-century fabrics. The stitches holding the irregular scraps of fabric together were so close and precise that not a raw edge showed. These functional stitches were sewn in a flame stitch pattern and glowed in their silkiness. The color range of both the stitches and the amazing antique fabrics reminded me of a Fabergé egg.

I also love the Italian cutwork with embroidery that I usually find in squares or rectangles, which makes me think they were window or door pelmets, or possibly a type of canopy, or even a table runner. Some of the fragile ones I have found are from the 17th century and are awaiting framing. Their rich red, blue, gold, and green velvets and silks have mellowed to softer colors. When repairing these, I often find the original strong color under the top layer of fabric. I sometimes feel like an archeologist of design trends, or at the very least, a detective.

Many of these textiles have been embroidered on silk and do not hold up well as pillows. They are exquisite when framed for conservation. I love to mount them on homespun linen because the contrast of the elegant embroidery against the rough texture of the hand-woven linen intensifies the beauty of each work. If I'm not framing this handmade artwork, I try to salvage a bit of embroidery or an appliqué, and reapply it to a more robust fabric. Early in my career, I bought several perfect pieces of 19th-century silk lampas from Lyon, France. This lampas was a thickly woven silk with a pattern of faces in a silvery-gold color. The perfect square fragments had been on the backs of chairs, hence their superb condition. The seats had been worn out completely and were irreparable. I was thrilled to have these chair backs that I could design so quickly and not have to apply the pattern myself. They seemed very sturdy, only to reveal that within a year, they would split when exposed to sun, air, and probably modern life. Since that blunder, I have avoided all silks that look like they are in good condition, and have focused on saving the embellishments from decaying materials.

**ABOVE** In this portrait from the 1880s, the famous French actress Sarah Bernhardt lounges pensively in romantic ruffles on a beautifully embroidered fabric draped over her divan.

**OPPOSITE** This glorious piece of silver metallic European embroidery shows incredible fish scale sequin work and silver cording couched to make leaf designs and edge the sequins. Found in France, it was just a large scrap and its previous life is a mystery.

**OVERLEAF** Eighteenth century gold and silver metallic embroidery appears to have been reapplied to a piece of 19th century red silk that hangs on the back of the settee in the living room. When I discovered it, someone had already removed some of the embellishments. The European cutwork, embroidery and appliqué piece on the seat is thought to be a 17th-century panel that could have adorned a bed. This piece is not a candidate for pillows because of its delicate and worn condition.

**OPPOSITE** A raised silver-metallic European fleur-de-lys embroidery has been bordered with an antique silver metallic galón on a persimmon-colored velvet. This symbol is found on many French articles and fabrics, as well as throughout the church. The European embroideries have a history of overlapping with the ecclesiastical embroideries. Many wealthy patrons who had elaborate needleworked garments or hangings gave them to the church after they were no longer needed in the secular world. These pieces were reworked into vestments, altar frontals, and many other liturgical garments and decorations.

**RIGHT 1.** Judging from the grapes and wheat in the embroidery, this lavish 19th century raised gold-metallic embroidery was most likely originally from an altar frontal. It had been reworked into another textile, so this is its third life. These long, glamorous pillows are beautiful on beds or in the middle of a sofa. **2.** A surprisingly modern six-petal flower design with scrolling leaves from an early 19th-century thickly raised embroidered appliqué makes a wondrous pillow. The bronze patina goes beautifully with the light greenish grey of the French blue velvet. **3.** This pillow has been embellished with one of the most extraordinary works I've ever found. The high-relief embroidery was very difficult to repair but was worth the effort. The elements from a long panel were rearranged to get a shorter composition. This textile could have originally been a panel from a church, was around the canopy of a bed, or on a window valence. **4.** This European embroidery is actually from a religious vestment. It is asymmetrical and does not have the grapes and wheat symbolism so often found in liturgical textiles. From an aesthetic view, since it was very busy, I had it reapplied by hand to a silver–colored velvet so that it was more monochromatic and textural. **5.** This lovely dusty lavender color was the perfect ground for this machine-made chain-stitched silver and cream embroidery from the early 20th century. It was removed from a disintegrating silk and sewn to its new velvet ground with the edges turned under. The antique silver metallic galón was repurposed and had the perfect patina and, fortunately, the perfect length.

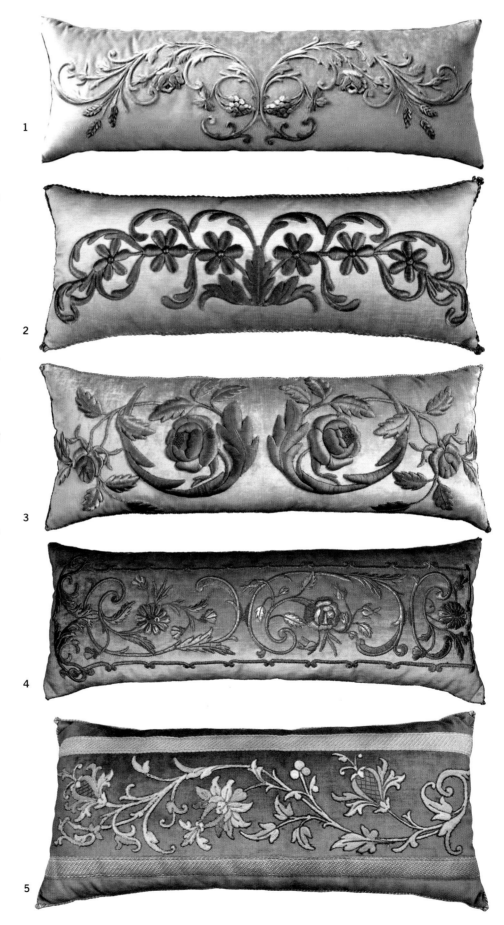

# TEXTILE CATEGORY: TAPESTRY

Tapestries truly awe me. When I stare at a tapestry in a museum I feel the same sensation as when I stare at the lake in front of our house. The mystery of unanswered questions bombards me. Who made you? How long did it take for you to be created? What was happening in history when you were produced? What have you witnessed in your lifetime? The good news is, you can learn a lot about the nuances of tapestries from museums, books, and the internet. But there is no substitute for seeing them in person.

Hand-loomed tapestries were produced in Europe from medieval times until the 1800s when technology created automated processes. The workshops were as varied as small Italian ateliers that didn't last long, to the large-scale high-quality production from Brussels that dominated the industry for long periods. Wars and religious persecution generated movement amongst the talented weavers, so tapestry production occurred in various areas of Europe, depending on the political climate.

Tapestries are woven from interlaced threads called a warp and a weft. The warp is the base and provides the tension, so that the colored weft can be woven back and forth between the warp threads. The design, or cartoon, is painted by an artist and positioned behind the tapestry so the weaver can follow the color and pattern. He is actually working from the backside of the tapestry. By the time it is finished, all of the warp threads are completely covered and the detailed picture emerges. Originally, tapestries were woven for the nobility and the church. Before the 18th century, these two groups were just about the only ones who could afford to commission such a labor-intensive undertaking. For example, a king liked to document his victorious battle, or a cathedral used tapestries to portray Biblical stories. In cold, large, drafty spaces, such as banquet halls or castle staircases, tapestries were not just for decoration, but also offered a form of insulation. With the economic rise of the merchant classes in the 18th century, a more generic type of tapestry composition began to appear, featuring a bucolic, wooded country scene, usually with a chateau or town in the background. These tapestries, with lots of foliage and greenery are often referred to as *verdure,* which comes from the French word "vert," green.

Verdure fragments as well as floral borders are my most common finds. When looking at handwoven tapestry fragments, an unusual subject matter catches my attention first. Pleasing colors and a repairable condition are important factors to consider. I love architectural fragments, figures, and animals. But I also love the greens and blues of the *verdure.* (Adding a *verdure* tapestry pillow to a room is like bringing in a plant you don't have to water.)

When designing tapestry pillows, I try to play up the actual antique fragment and not overly embellish the pillow with new passementerie. I find that the antique textiles' colors have usually faded to a hue that new trims overwhelm. I like to finish them with an aged metallic ribbon called galón or galloon, so that the composition is more clean-lined and the pure tapestry is celebrated.

**ABOVE** The engraving shows weavers at the Manufacture Nationale des Gobelins, the renowned French tapestry manufacturer that can still be found at the same location in Paris' 13th *arrondissement.* Multiple colors of threads dangle on bobbins and display the number of colors being woven by hand.

**OPPOSITE** A detail of a late-16th century antique Flemish tapestry fragment portrays Ceres, the goddess of agriculture. The wheat motif, the flora in her hair, and the scythe in her hand are clues to her identity.

**OVERLEAF** Most likely from the Royal Manufacture of Aubusson, France, and dating from about 1720, this tapestry panel of a soldier hangs over the back of a chair on the upstairs landing of our house, its colors resonating with those in the 19th century Swedish secretary. The curtains are bordered in a Greek key design from my hand-painted fabric collection by Coleman Taylor Textiles.

**OPPOSITE** Architectural elements make up some of my most cherished tapestry pillows. The symmetry is particularly nice in this mid-17th century example, most likely from Brussels. So often, when finding a worn tapestry fragment, the subject is not centered or is partially damaged beyond repair. This makes symmetrical images and pairs more difficult to achieve.

**RIGHT 1.** I love the design of the eight-pointed star on this antique tapestry fragment. The aged gold-metallic galón has a pattern that mimics the shape of the tapestry composition. The nautical star shares a likeness with the imagery of an old map. **2.** The cherub on the cartouche overlooking a beautiful landscape is one of my treasured antique tapestry finds. This pillow embodies my favorite elements—faces, architecture, and the greens and blues of the landscape. **3.** This pillow is most likely a late-16th century Flemish tapestry border fragment that depicts fruits, vegetables, and foliage cascading over a garden structure in an abundant display. The blues, greens, creams, and gold shades of this gorgeous remnant go perfectly with its antique gold-metallic galón frame. **4.** A 17th-century Flemish tapestry piece features figures festooned with drapery. To finish it, I used the antique silver serpentine galón for a border because I felt that the swags of fabric in this tapestry echoed the curves in the trim. **5.** A verdure fragment from a 17th- or 18th-century Aubusson tapestry has the typical green foliage for which it is named. The pillow, with its shades of greens, blues, browns, and creams, is framed with an understated dark galón. **6.** The figure of the French man was salvaged from an 18th-century Aubusson fragment. This pillow is framed by a galón with a patina that doesn't pull attention away from the scene. **7.** I am not sure of the origins of this hand-woven tapestry fragment but the weaving is more primitive, with less technical shading. I like fragments with faces and architectural elements, even when the artistry is more naive. I purchased the textile in Paris, for what was one of my early tapestry pillows. **8.** This tapestry was probably woven in Brussels, due to its high quality. Artists from all over Europe were hired to paint the cartoons—the designs for the tapestries. But the most prolific weaving came from the area of the southern Netherlands, so is often referred to as Flemish.

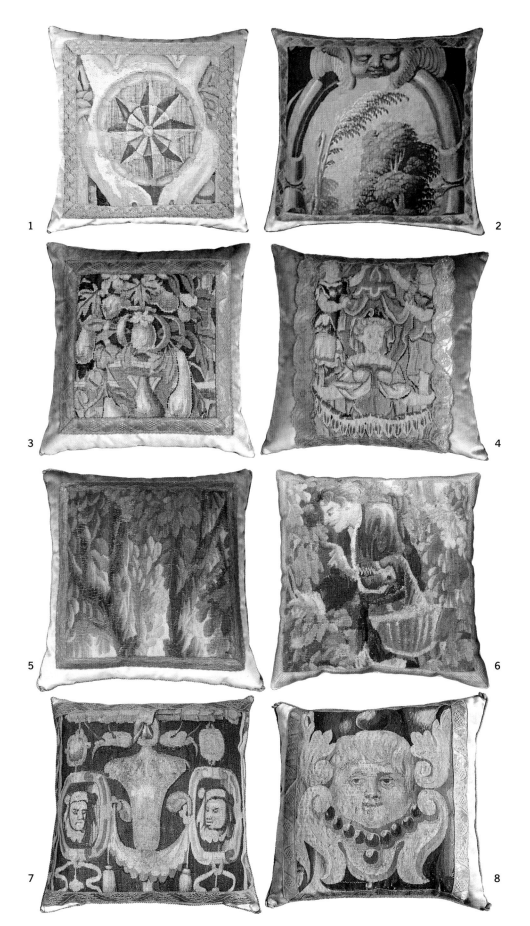

Most of the Ottoman Empire raised-gold or -silver metal embroidery I use for my pillows dates from the end of the 19th century to the early 20th century. I particularly love the juxtaposition of the more primitive stitches with the elegant glint of the gold and silver threads. The thickness of these designs is normally created by stitching over leather or cardboard. The dival stitch is used so that only the gold threads lie on top of the leather or cardboard and are held in position by another thread that catches it from underneath. They are often finished with delicate couching around the design. The motifs I commonly find are typical Turkish flowers such as tulips, carnations, hyacinths, and roses. There are also stitches depicting pomegranates, apples, artichokes, baskets, scrollwork, and vines. The elegant monograms of a Sultan in Islamic calligraphy, called *tughras,* are also fairly easy to find at flea markets.

Most of these embroideries were created on dark navy, black, red, or burgundy grounds and I found myself having trouble selling those colors as pillows and worrying that the antique velvet or silk grounds would not hold up over time. It finally dawned on me to cut around this beautiful handwork with tiny, sharp cuticle scissors and reapply the salvaged embroidery by hand sutures to sturdier, more decorative colored fabrics, such as velvet or homespun linens. I also like to rearrange these embroidered elements to create more modern designs, or take the floating *boteh,* a tear-shaped abstract floral motif and make patterns for my pillows.

Over time, I have accumulated an extensive collection of antique metallic threads in different patinas that we use to repair these embroideries. Many of these stitched decorations come from a caftan-like robe called a *bindalli,* which means "a thousand branches." (And should mean thousands of stitches.) These robes were worn by brides and their female family and friends during wedding festivities, and given by sultans to worthy citizens as robes of honor. A family would often cut a *bindalli* into sections so that each child could inherit a piece of their family history. Another source for this beautiful *dival* metal embroidery is the *Bohça,* which is a square cloth used for wrapping gifts or items. This tradition is thought to have started with the nomadic Turks, who bundled their possessions in decorated fabrics every time they moved. These fantastic embroideries were far reaching in their range of styles and skills, and were created in guilds by professional male embroiderers as well as domestically and, in a few Istanbul workshops, by female needle workers.

**ABOVE** An 1882 illustration of a sultan and a sultana in 16th-century Ottoman regalia. The colors and textures of the garments show the skill of the early Ottoman Empire weavers and embroiderers.

**OPPOSITE** The raised embroidery, made of silk rather than the usual metallic threads, is one of the most unusual Middle Eastern textiles I have ever found. The Parisian vendor I bought it from thought it was 19th-century Egyptian. The stylized vining flowers are characteristic of Islamic art, and it is rare to find silk embroidery in such good condition.

**OVERLEAF** An antique cream and gold work cape and an ottoman jacket with *dival* embroidery hang in the master bedroom. These garments are not for the cutting table but, rather, to be worn on special occasions. There are also records of guilds and workshops that produced these luxurious garments as a commercial industry. The Italian drawings are of Ceres, who, with the wheat in her hair, will bring good luck to the cotton harvest.

**OPPOSITE** After a week of falling in love with Istanbul, I stopped in Paris on my way home to search for European fragments. One of my favorite vendors at the Marché Dauphine had this vintage souvenir embroidered pillow with the image of Hagia Sophia, the former Greek Orthodox church in Istanbul, converted into a mosque, now a museum. I cut away the worn silk back and framed the front with a European silver antique galón in a vining leaf pattern that evoked for me an arabesque style.

**RIGHT 1.** This textile, similar to examples I have found in Turkey, Paris, Parma in Italy, and even Houston, I was told was a popular mid-20th century Egyptian or Syrian cushion cover. **2.** This unusual French piece seems to have European-style stitched leaves, but the crescent reminds me of the Ottoman Empire. **3.** The triangular shape of the embroidery indicates that it came from the corner of an elaborately embroidered *bohça*, or wrapping cloth from Turkey. **4.** The tighter and more delicate stitches of this *dival* embroidery lead me to believe the distressed caftan from which it was removed belonged to a prominent person. The scrollwork's arms were moved up to make a pleasing composition. **5.** This circular design came from the center of a 19th-century *bohça* found in Istanbul. The padded gold-metallic *dival* stitch is held in place by a thread coming up from underneath. The metallic stitches are caught from underneath, at the edges of the design, and make a three-dimensional pattern by laying satin stitches side by side over the padding. **6.** This pillow shows another central design from an Ottoman *bohça*, but in a silver-metallic *dival* stitch. The pattern was removed from a distressed black velvet ground and sewn onto a new, sturdier velvet. **7.** This pale chartreuse velvet is perfect for the large gold-metallic embroidered bow from a late-19th century or early-20th century Ottoman caftan. Without the tassel and the *dival* stitch, this design could have been European. I had the galón finished in a ribbonwork technique, where the edge of the trim is loosely stitched and then pulled tight to create the circles in the corners. **8.** A corner decoration from a square *bohça* makes a beautiful pillow. Since the triangle shape of the raised *dival* embroidery is wider than it is tall, I added the strips of antique galón to make the pillow into a square.

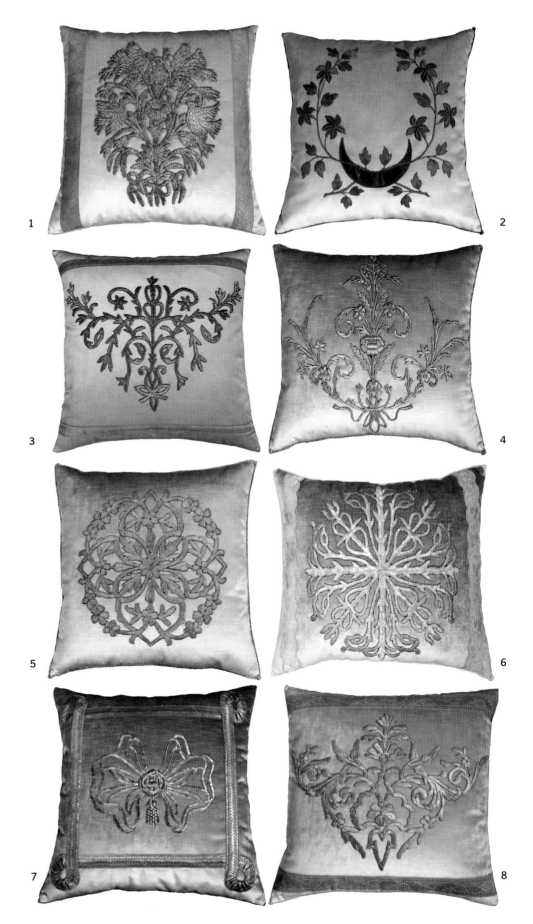

1  2  3  4  5  6  7  8

# TEXTILE CATEGORY: HOMESPUN

The many textures and subtle shades of homespun linen draw me to them like a magnet. I love the feel of this material both visually and tactilely. The contrast of the refined European embroideries and raised metallic work with the nubby texture of homemade linen allows for the creation of wonderful pillows. I like to back my antique toiles with homespun linen, and simple pillows with the exposed imperfect handmade selvages are very special. Also, the texture makes a sublime background for framing distressed fragments that are too delicate to be used for pillows.

Linen is made from the fibers of the flax plant. Flax was thought to have been first domesticated from a wild variety in ancient Mesopotamia, which is often called the cradle of civilization. Handwoven linen has been used for wrapping mummies in Egyptian tombs.

The homespun linens I find are mostly from France and Germany, and are approximately 80 to 120 years old. They were typically woven on handmade looms by rural European farm families. They used this linen for trade, clothing, bedding, and grain sacks. (The stripe on many of the grain sacks helped to identify the family's harvest, so the miller could return them to their rightful owner.) This type of rustic fabric was used primarily by the poor, and very few articles of clothing have survived because of the wear and tear of daily use. The American colonists imported the flax seeds from Europe, and linen was produced in many remote areas, where self-sufficiency was the key to survival. The grade varied tremendously and depended on the variety of the seed, the growing climate, and the skill of the weaver.

It took months of backbreaking labor to complete the process of growing the flax and preparing it for weaving. I've also read that it took a woman up to six hours to produce just a single yard of this aptly named fabric that was always spun at home. Often, it was the unmarried woman in the family who would spin the threads, hence the origin of the word "spinster."

**ABOVE** Scutching—or dressing the flax—which is part of the long, tedious process of making homespun linen from the flax plant, Linum has been depicted in this delightful engraving from the *Great Industries of Great Britain,* produced in London in 1880.

**OPPOSITE** This vintage set of homespun towels with its charming cross-stitched initials has survived many a casual meal as table napkins in the Vizard household. Homespun linen from the flax plant is an amazingly durable material.

**OVERLEAF** A vignette on the swing of our upstairs screened-in porch shows hardy homespun linens airing out in the lake breeze.

**PAGES 130–131** Pillows of homespun linen share the playhouse with the vintage painted ducks that were done by a World War II soldier in the 1940s.

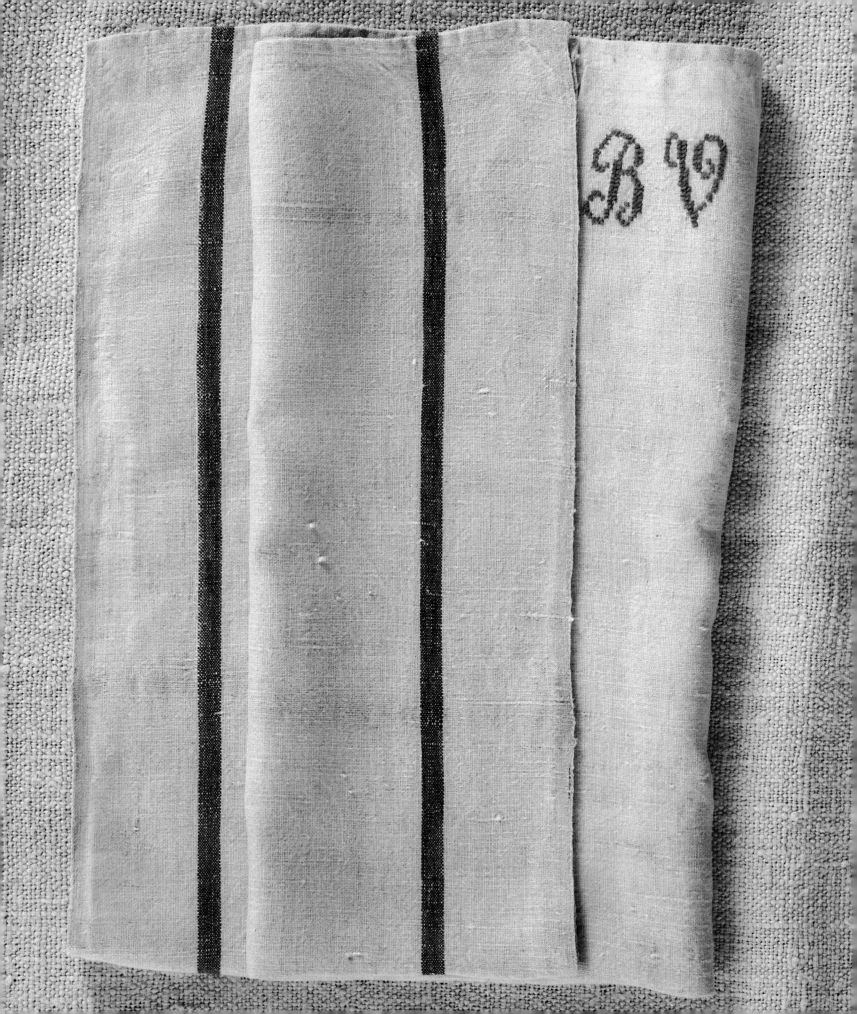

**OPPOSITE** I love the contrast of the nubby homespun linen with the sophisticated Ottoman Empire raised gold-metallic *dival* embroidery on this pillow. The antique gold strips of galón complete the composition, and the hand-trimmed vintage military cording is knotted in the corners, illustrating one of our signature finishes.

**RIGHT 1.** This unusual high-relief embroidery of a bee was taken from the scraps of an early-20th century French banner. I love the austere quality of the detailed gold work on the white texture of the homespun linen—as if the bee were flying over the cotton fields outside the studio. **2.** A metallic appliqué depicts the head of a buck. I bordered the motif with an antique silver-metallic galón for a slightly larger pillow. **3.** The blue and faded red stripe of this homespun linen pillow is significant. Many families wove a different colored stripe into their homespun material so that the grain sacks from which they were created would be identifiable. After receiving the delivery of the grain, the miller would know whom to return the valuable hand-crafted sack to for the next harvest. I left the beautifully finished selvage edges exposed on the pillow's sides. **4.** The juxtaposition of this ornate European gold-metallic embroidery with the coarse homespun linen is unexpected, casual, yet elegant. I like these pillows to accent a monochromatic room with touches of gold leaf highlighting picture frames and other hard surfaces.
**5.** The smooth, modern lines of this 19th-century quatre-foil shape contrast nicely with the 1920s natural-colored homespun linen. I framed the silver embroidered quatrefoil with antique silver-metallic galón to increase the pillow's size, and finished it with a vintage hand-sewn cording knotted in the corners. **6.** A simple frame of antique silver serpentine galón dresses up the understated homespun linen pillow. **7.** This 1920s shiny silver cloth of gold appliqué has been couched around the perimeter with gold cording. Found on a French banner, I felt the appliqué would be too showy for a velvet ground.
**8.** A late 18th- or early-19th-century toile fragment blends beautifully with the color and texture of the linen—a good marriage because most antique toile fragments I have found have many a hole that I have to work around. The homespun makes a wonderful base with which to frame these lovely French copper-printed scenes.

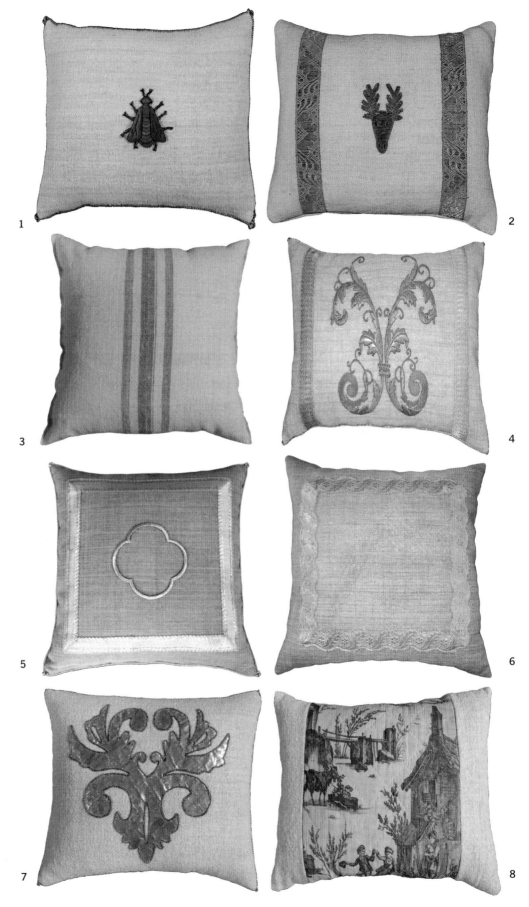

1
2
3
4
5
6
7
8

133

I hate having to say goodbye to a pillow, especially if it's one of my favorites, but I love to see them in their final havens in the pages of magazines and books. Thank you to the many talented interior designers who have chosen to include them in their chic projects.

**OPPOSITE** Lady Cynthia Mary Evelyn Asquith, the English writer known for her ghost stories and diaries, charmingly rests her arm on a pillow in the 1914 watercolor by Edmund Dulac (1882-1953).

**LEFT** A Middle Eastern goldwork pillow functions as the perfect piece of jewelry in this atmospheric foyer by Susan Ferrier of McAlpine, Booth & Ferrier's design office in Atlanta, Georgia. The dramatic painting is by Michael Dines, an Atlanta-based artist. The lantern is from Dennis and Leen in Los Angeles, California. The Mountain Brook, Alabama, home was inspired by the neighborhood's 1920's English-style construction and is by architects Bobby McAlpine and Scott Torode.

**OPPOSITE** The clean lines of a blue velvet pillow with silver-metallic European embroidery harmonize beautifully with the watery palette of this Manhattan apartment by James and Phoebe Howard. Based between Jacksonville, Florida, and Atlanta, Georgia, the couple works across the country, but not often together. In this rare joint venture, Phoebe was responsible for the softer elements, such as the beautiful fabrics, while Jim determined the furniture layout.

**RIGHT** Gerrie Bremermann, a master of mixing contemporary with antique furnishings, used one of our tapestry pillows and a French ribbonwork cushion in this lovely Palm Beach interior. Gerrie was the first designer to buy my pillows in 1994, and has been carrying them ever since then in her exquisite shop fronting her design business on Magazine Street in New Orleans, Louisiana.

**LEFT** I love the unexpected juxtaposition of the contemporary
1960s art by Al Held and the
golden yellow and blue pillow
created from an 18th-century
ecclesiastical embroidery in this
interior by designer Renea
Abbott, owner of Shabby Slips in
Houston, Texas. The gold leaf
touches on the Louis XIV settee
make the antique textile pillow
sparkle. The wool rug is from
Creative Flooring Resources and,
with the white walls and crisp
Belgian linen, gives the room a
modern sensibility.

**OPPOSITE** A cushion created
from an 18th century gold and
chocolate Portuguese appliqué
on silver velvet creates a daz-
zling focus in this living room by
Houston-based designer Katie
Scott. The sparkle from the
brass of the Lucite coffee table
is also picked up in the pillow
and gold-leaf accents throughout
the living room of this contemporary Houston house.

**OPPOSITE** Barry Dixon, the Warrenton, Virginia-based interior designer, blends this understated aged, gold appliqué torch on a pale French blue velvet pillow, with the sumptuous Delfino Fortuny draperies. The Farrow & Ball Venetian plaster and the Rose Tarlow chair enhance the luxurious McClean, Virginia, dressing room.

**RIGHT** The texture and color of this early 20th-century chain-stitched embroidery from India is repeated in the antique Italian cabinet from Randall Tysinger Antiques. The Chevy Chase, Maryland, home, by Dixon, is a global mix that showcases the Moroccan antique jars and the collection of Italian intaglio. The walls were hand-painted by Warnock Studios. The sofa, from Dixon's collection for Tomlinson/Erwin-Lambeth, has been upholstered in a Donghia fabric.

**OVERLEAF LEFT** A pillow embellished with a 19th-century Ottoman Empire metallic embroidery, removed from a *bohça*, punctuates this interior by Annelle Primos of Jackson, Mississippi. The Turkish *dival* stitch shows the skill involved in this intricate art.

**OVERLEAF RIGHT** Known for her subtle use of color and detail, Primos chose blue velvet pillows with antique Ottoman Empire raised embroidery to mirror the colors of the painting.

**LEFT** From my line of hand-painted fabrics by Coleman Taylor Textiles, these crisp white and silvery gold Greek key pillows echo the texture of the modern white leather chair in a New Orleans sunroom by Gerrie Bremermann. The segmented mirror backdrop not only reflects light and the sparkling crystal chandelier, but makes the space feel twice as grand.

**OPPOSITE** These early B.Viz Design pillows flaunt a delicate gold appliqué of a flower and a cloth of gold damask on a funky late-18th century walnut Venetian sofa in the Houston shop of Watkins Culver. The peeling green and cyan blue walls, painted by the artist Jay Larussi, have been a signature at this shop of curiosities and antiques for over 20 years.

**OPPOSITE** New Orleans designer Hal Williamson fuses antique maps of Paris with colorful ikat fabrics and a bright Oushak rug in publishing executive and writer Debra Shriver's informal sitting room that overlooks a courtyard in the French Quarter. Williamson incorporates a little sparkle from a B.Viz Design goldwork pillow, and faded antique Fortuny pillow with red and gold-metallic galón.

**RIGHT** I fell in love with the hand-drawn design of an unstitched needlepoint canvas at an antiques fair on one of my trips to Lyon, France. The graphic quality of the drawing and the texture of the perfectly aged open-weave canvas inspired some of my favorite pillows. Atlanta-based interior designer Suzanne Kasler placed this unusual pillow in an entrance hall with its surprising use of wallpaper on the ceiling that mirrors the texture of the jute rug.

**LEFT** This pillow with its subtle antique silver-metallic flower appliqué has a simple, modern design, to which I've added an antique galón with the same patina. It sits on a French painted settee from Bremermann Design in Jennifer Rabalais' New Orleans house. She is the owner of Jade, a local home furnishings shop.

**OPPOSITE** Textural homespun linen pillows with small, antique embroidered deer heads removed from a vintage French banner accent the elegant Connecticut living room of New York designer Matthew Patrick Smyth.

**OVERLEAF LEFT** A pillow made from a piece of vintage gold brocade framed with an antique galón lends a soft touch to the linear repetition of the books in a wonderful Bethesda, Maryland, library by interior designer Barry Dixon.

**OVERLEAF RIGHT** *Milieu Magazine* publisher and designer Pam Pierce of Houston styled this chic vignette showcasing my acid-green Fortuny pillows with a wonderful vintage pink suzani pillow. The Uzbek hand-embroidered suzani was a rare find at the Grand Bazaar in Istanbul. The perfect foil is the textural modern art created with hand-cut rag paper by Michael Buscemi, who is represented through Ann Connelly Fine Art in Baton Rouge, Louisiana.

**LEFT** I bought this intricate chain-stitched embroidered su-zani in Turkey, even though it was machine-made, because I responded to its colors and the pattern. Melissa Rufty, who is originally from South Carolina, now owns MMR Interiors in New Orleans, masterfully placed it in this sculptural antique Biedermeier chair. The natural turtle shells hang like art on a creamy lacquered wall in an uptown New Orleans home.

**OPPOSITE** In this glamorous powder room on the Upper East Side of Manhattan, William Sofield of Studio Sofield, Inc., a New York firm, placed a striking antique Portuguese cutwork and appliqué pillow on a chic Fortuny fabric-upholstered bench.

**RIGHT** New York-based Courtney Coleman and William Brockschmidt get a punch of color from the bright pillows made from an Uzbek suzani I found just outside the Grand Bazaar in Istanbul, Turkey. The snappy Quadrille stripe on the Regency chair and the Roman shades by Kay Neal Draperies are the perfect foils for the pillows. The duck cloth upholstery piping mimics the stripe's colors.

**OVERLEAF** One of my earliest clients, Mary Jane Ryburn, a former *Veranda* editor, is an ardent textile aficionado from Dallas, Texas. This interesting living area alludes to her love of travel, and tendency for collecting the unusual. The long pillow on the Queen Anne sofa is fashioned from a priest's antique stole that was worn around the neck. The vintage suzani, covering the round table in the corner, gives the room a perfect punch of color. The large piece over the sofa is from an opera set design and depicts the Duomo in Florence, Italy.

**PREVIOUS PAGES LEFT** In this Texas lakeside retreat, Dallas-based designer Shannon Bowers uses a pop of tribal style with one of my favorite Fortuny patterns, Melilla in beige and brown. The modern design is an early Fortuny pattern inspired by Java, in Indonesia. This living room's peaceful palette and use of patina makes it a welcome respite from the city.

**PREVIOUS PAGES RIGHT** A pair of Carnavalet Fortuny pillows with our signature hand-stitched metallic cording knotted in the corners pops the colors of the tulips in this Houston living room, by designer Eleanor Cummings. The dominating antique Italian painting from Watkins Culver sets a religious tone for the room. The antique Italian sofa is recovered in a heavy Rogers & Goffigon linen.

**RIGHT** The timeless appeal of Fortuny fabrics shows in this subtly hand-printed textile that holds its own in a contemporary environment. The Connecticut living room is by the New York-based Bruce Glickman and his partner Wilson Henley. They own Duane Modern, a Manhattan shop that specializes in decorative mid-century modern design, and also offers their own line of furniture.

**OPPOSITE** I love the unexpected pairing of the casual soft blue buffalo check on the 19th-century French chairs with the 17th-century tapestry-fragment pillows and Regency commode. Gerrie Bremermann's classic design permeates this venerable uptown New Orleans gem of a home.

**RIGHT** Houston-based designer Eleanor Cummings had this magnificent bed custom-made from an old architectural fragment. The lamp, from Paris, sits on an antique Louis XVI chest. The pillow was created from an early 20th-century clerical cope fragment found in France. This elegant bedroom is dappled with gold accents, from the touches of gold leaf and brass hardware to the gold-metallic embroidered vining flowers of the long pillow.

**LEFT** In a pièd-a-terre in the historic French Quarter of New Orleans, Los Angeles-based designer Tom Landry mixes B.Viz pillows with the charm of toile in his bedroom. The color and shape of the aged metallic-silver embroidery is echoed in the pattern. The simple antique galón-framed pillow echoes the shape of the framed artwork.

**OPPOSITE** A pillow decorated with Ottoman Empire raised silver-metallic embroidery takes center stage in the master bedroom in a model residence designed by New York-based interior designer Scott Sanders for the Printing House, a loft building in Lower Manhattan. Turquoise walls help create a serene retreat, and act as a backdrop for a luxurious cream linen-upholstered bed. The painting above the bed is *Horsey Love* by New York artist David Humphrey.

**LEFT** A long pillow embellished with rescued and restored vintage embroidery from a priest's vestment makes the king-sized bed feel more cozy in this Jackson, Mississippi, bedroom by Annelle Primos. The raised goldwork harmonizes with the gold medallion decoration on the iron bed.

**OPPOSITE** New Orleans lighting designer Julie Neill used an asymmetrical Turkish embroidered pillow as an adornment for the custom-designed bed that was made in her local workshop. The feather light fixtures are a fun accent and lend a nice textural contrast.

**OVERLEAF** Melissa Rufty's daughter's bedroom is emboldened with the daring use of the hand-crafted black-and-white basma or satin-stitched suzani pillows. The beds are dressed in crisp monogrammed Leontine Linens.

**LEFT** Late-17th or early-18th century *verdure* tapestry pillows recall the patina of the smoky antique mirror in this timeless Atlanta bedroom by designer Barbara Westbrook. The iron bed is custom-made for Westbrook Interiors and the bench is from BD Jeffries, also of Atlanta. The unusual mirror is from Linda Horsley Antiques in Atlanta.

This book tells my story of accomplishment against all odds, and offers the textile information I sought so many years ago. After reading many volumes of textile books and traveling to countless museums and flea markets, this glossary is a wonderful basic course and the manual I wish I'd had back in my early days.

**OPPOSITE** An 1837 color lithograph of a Greek girl from *Illustrations of Constantinople* is the work of the 19th century Orientalist, English painter John Frederick Lewis.

## ABHLA BHARAT
Mirror-work embroidery from Kathiawar (India), in which round pieces of mirror are buttonholed or used in conjunction with stem or close herringbone stitch.

## ACANTHUS
A stylized leaf ornament based on the Mediterranean acanthus plant, which is often seen in classical architecture. It is one of the most widely used ornamental forms in the decorative arts.

## ADRAS
Glossy fabric, half silk and half cotton, usually made with narrow stripes and a beetled finish. Made in India & Central Asia. Suzani patterns are often stitched on this type of fabric.

## AESTHETIC MOVEMENT
A reform design movement that occurred during the 1860s and 1870s. The style was influenced by Japanese decoration, late-17th and early-18th century domestic design, and blue and white Chinese porcelain. Simple forms and uncluttered surfaces were a reaction to the highly elaborate products of mainstream Victorian taste and ornament was often symmetrical. Typical motifs included were sunflowers, fan shapes, peacock feathers, and bamboo.

## AGNUS DEI
The Lamb of God symbol, used in ecclesiastical embroidery, depicts a lamb holding a Christian flag.

## ALB
A sleeved ankle-length tunic, usually white linen (symbolic of Christ's linen shroud), worn by the celebrant of the Mass either with a stole or under other vestments. The first appearance of the liturgical alb was probably in the 9th century.

## ALTAR FRONTAL
Piece of rich fabric, generally embroidered, that hangs from a rod or is mounted on a frame in front of the altar. It is also called an antependium.

## AMICE
An oblong piece of cloth, usually white linen, which can also be elaborately embroidered, worn by the celebrant around the neck and shoulders and partly under the alb. In their early appearances, amices were frequently worn as head coverings. Much later, the amice became a collar, worn like a scarf.

## ANTEPENDIUM
See ALTAR FRONTAL

## ANTHEMION
A stylized, classical floral motif based on a honeysuckle that was much used in the Neoclassical period, usually as a repeating ornament. It closely resembles a palmette.

## APPLIQUÉ
Fabric or any type of material that is cut out and sewn, embroidered, or fastened to another fabric. Also referred to as applied work.

## ARABESQUE
An ornamental design consisting of intertwined flowing lines, scrollwork, or flowers and leaves that originated in the Near East.

## ARBORESCENT DESIGN
A pattern that resembles or is based on a tree.

## ART NOUVEAU
A decorative style that was popular in Europe from the 1890's to around 1910. The designs were based on sinuous curves, flowing lines, organic forms, and asymmetry. The motifs often incorporated flowers, leaves, and insect motifs.

## ART DECO
A style of ornament popular in the 1920's and 1930's. In embroidery, it was expressed by a stylized rendering of the human form, flowers, and other objects with a strong accent on texture. This involved the use of various thicknesses of thread in one piece of work, coarse ground fabrics, and sharply contrasting and even clashing colors.

## ARTS AND CRAFTS MOVEMENT
Led by British designer William Morris, in the 19th and early 20th century, in contrast to the machine-made processes of the Industrial Revolution, it advocated a return to simplicity and functionalism in design and quality of materials and craftsmanship.

## ASSISI EMBROIDERY
Type of embroidery originating in Assisi, northern Italy, which is characterized by the design being left plain and the background filled in. Because the designs are often heraldic and only one color is used, usually red or blue, the work has a very formal and dignified look.

## ATELIER
A workshop or studio, but can also be described as a place where fine sewing and embroidery is done; for example, the workrooms of couture houses.

## AUBUSSON
Fine, hand-woven tapestry used for wall hangings or carpets. Named after the famous French village where they were originally made.

## AUREOLE
A radiance that surrounds the head or the whole figure in the representation of a sacred person and is often embroidered with gold threads. Halo.

## AURICULAR STYLE
Thought to be originally based on the shape of the human ear, it was a style popular in Northern Europe during the 16th and 17th century and was characterized by undulating and rippling effects.

## BADLA
Gold or silver-gilt thread that is used in Indian metal-thread embroidery.

## BAROQUE
Originating in Italy, a heavily sculptural late 17th- and early 18th-century classically based style found in architecture, furniture, and other objects incorporating an extravagant use of plant forms such as the acanthus, human forms such as putti, and other motifs set in curvaceous shapes, often making use of strongly contradicting tones and colors.

## BASKET WEAVE
A tabby weave using two or more threads so as to give a basket-like effect to fabric. Basketweave fabric is used for certain types of embroidery. In America, basket weave is the term for diagonal tent stitch.

## BATIK
A method of resist dyeing that employs wax as the resist. The pattern is covered in wax and the fabric is then dyed. (The waxed patterns will not take the dye.) Wax is then removed by boiling the fabric, applying solvent, or by ironing over an absorbent substrate. Batik dyeing originated in Indonesia.

## BATTLEMENTED
Shaped like battlements of a church or castle. Effect is achieved in needlework by cutting the fabric and using an edging stitch, by favoring the shape or by applying braid in this shape.

## BAUDEKIN
One of the richest fabrics of the Middle Ages, made of silk interwoven with threads of gold, and used by royalty, nobility, and the church.

## BAUHAUS
German school of architecture that aimed to create prototype designs for mass-produced everyday items, using austere, geometric forms, and modern materials such as tubular steel and plastics. Its functional approach came out of the Arts and Crafts Movement and led to Modernism.

## BAYEUX TAPESTRY
The most important piece of embroidery in the world. Although called a tapestry, it is more properly embroidery, since it was worked with a needle and wool on linen and is not tapestry-woven. It is 231 feet wide and 19.5 inches tall and depicts the events leading up to the battle of Hastings, when William the Conqueror defeated Harold of England in 1066, the battle itself and the death of Harold. The stitches are stem and outline, with laid couched work, and in contrast to the rather formal metal-thread embroideries typical of this date, it appears rather lively.

## BEADING
Outlining, highlighting patterns or depicting a picture on material by stitching beads to it. Also the term refers to making jewelry with beads.

## BERLIN WOOL
Berlin wool work is a style of embroidery similar to today's needlepoint. It was typically executed with wool yarn on canvas and is usually worked in a single stitch, such as tent stitch. The design of such embroidery was often brightly colored because of the discovery in the 1830s of aniline dyes, which produced more vivid colors.

## BINDALLI
A heavily embroidered Turkish garment made for special occasions and weddings, and worn by the bride and her female family and friends. The metallic padded or raised embroidery was done in the dival stitch, which did not pierce the fabric but was attached to the surface only. Bindalli means "a thousand branches," which is indicative of its branching and stylized floral patterns. These velvet, caftan-like garments were also given as a gifts by the Sultan to visiting dignitaries and important citizens.

## BLOCK PRINTING
Hand-printing process where the motifs have been carved on wooden blocks. The dye is applied to the fabric from these blocks in a procedure similar to the rubber stamp technique.

## BOHÇA
A silk or velvet embroidered square cloth that was used to wrap or bundle items in Turkey. This tradition of wrapping items in cloth most likely stems from the early nomadic culture in Turkey's history. Decorated with dival embroidery, the bohça was also used to wrap important gifts or store precious keepsakes.

## BOKHARA (SUZANI STYLE)
City in Uzbekistan that has always been

known for its embroideries. Designs are often of formalized flowers, singly or in a bunch, worked in colored silks on linen.

## BOTEH
A leaf-shaped or pine cone motif derived from 17th-century Persian and Indian textiles. It was the inspiration for the paisley design.

## BOUCLÉ
An irregular, loopy yarn made by twisting heavier, pre-twisted threads around a fine core yarn.

## BROCADE
An all-over interwoven design, usually of figures or flowers, from a jacquard weave. It is accentuated with varying surfaces of color, and often metallic threads. The pattern is evident only on one side.

## BROCATELLE
A stiff, heavy fabric similar in appearance to brocade but with high relief. The filler yarns give it an embossed look. Originally, it was made to imitate Italian tooled leather The heavily figured cloth is most often made of a combination of silk, linen or wool. It is a jacquard weave fabric and can have strands of silver or gold highlighting its weave and complementing its patterns. In contrast, damask fabric traditionally employs a monochromatic theme.

## BUCKRAM
In the Middle Ages, a fine, soft cotton or linen fabric, but now a stiff pasted or gummed cloth used chiefly for interlining household articles such as pelmets and valences, and for stiffening embroideries.

## BUGLE
Small tube-shaped bead of transparent glass.

## BUGLE WORK
The attaching of bugles to a fabric by means of waxed thread and surface stitchery. Beads massed to give three-dimensional effect.

## BULLION EMBROIDERY
All types of embroidery worked entirely with metal threads. Also called auriphrygium.

## BYZANTINE EMBROIDERY
Combination of couched outlines, applied work, and fancy stitches dating from 1878, and useful for ornamenting thick materials. Shapes traced on the ground fabric are outlined by couching thick threads; other shapes are cut out in various fabrics and applied, again with a couched edge. Any space left in the pattern can be filled with variety of stitches.

## CABOCHON FOUNDATIONS
Small dome-shaped coarse foam or buckram forms used as centers for flowers or ornaments.

## CAFTAN (KAFTAN)
Long outer garment shaped like a coat, with straight, loose sleeves, and generally fastened with a sash. Worn in many places including North Africa, India, and the Middle East, and is frequently embroidered, especially from neck to waist.

## CALENDAR
To smooth or glaze paper or fabric by passing through heavy rollers.

## CARTOUCHE
A decorative motif in the shape of a sheet of paper with scrolling ends. French for scroll.

## CELTIC STYLE
Decorated style associated with Celtic peoples who spread from central Europe to Spain, Italy, and Britain around 2500 BCE. It incorporates curvilinear patterns, especially interlacing knots, with stylized animals and human forms. Inspirations for Art Nouveau design.

## CHASUBLE
A sleeveless outer vestment usually worn by the priest officiating at the Eucharist. Derives from the Roman paenula, a circular garment with a hole for the head, worn as a traveling cloak.

## CHENILLE
A novelty yarn with a nubby surface, which creates a soft hand when woven into fabric. Origin: French, chenille—caterpillar.

## CHENILLE WORK
Embroidery with chenille. The nubby thread is suitable for almost any description of embroidery.

## CHEVRON
Shape made when two beams meet at an angle at the roof. In needlework, the word is used to describe a stitch, a pattern sometimes woven into tweed and other materials, and a shape used in embroidery design.

## CHINTZ
First imported to Europe from India in the 17th century. A plain-weave, cotton fabric printed in multi color. Often, but not necessarily, in a glazed finish. Origin: Sanskrit word meaning spotted.

## CHI-RHO
Frequently used in ecclesiastical embroidery, the first two letters of the

Greek word for Christ, made into a monogram, used by early Christians as a symbol of their religion, as they easily formed a cross, and could be interpreted as pax, the Latin term for peace.

## CHROMO EMBROIDERY
Type of work of the late 19th century, used by the inexperienced or diffident embroiderer who doubted her capacity to shade or color correctly. Thin paper of the required color was tacked to the fabric and worked over in satin stitch with a matching thread. Finished article was not washable, as the paper was left in.

## CLOTH OF GOLD OR SILVER
Fabric, generally of silk, with some gold threads woven in. (Silver—fabric woven with silver threads, sometimes mixed with gold.) One of the richest fabrics ever made, and used for both garments and hangings when a great display of wealth or status was needed.

## COMPOUND WEAVE
General term for a fabric structure that is more complicated than a basic weave. It is composed of multiple sets of warps and/or wefts, each with different functions, creating a juxtaposition of textures within the fabric to highlight the design elements within a foreground and background, or the introduction of multiple colors.

## CONVENT INFLUENCE
Through the ages, learning and patient craftsmanship were taking place in convents throughout Europe. Whether through piety or status seeking, rich embroideries were required by church and state. It was usually from the convents that they were ordered, though there were secular embroideries and even secular schools of embroidery available. Through exploration and missionary work, religious groups emigrated, spreading innumerable types of embroidery throughout the world, and it became known as convent work or nuns' work.

## CO-OPERATIVE EMBROIDERY
Large pieces of needlework done by more than one person.

## COPE
Ecclesiastical outer garment or cloak, derived from the ordinary protective garment of Greeks and Romans.

## CORD
Form of rope of various thickness, made from twisted strands of any fiber.

## COTTON
Name for a wide variety of different fabrics and sewing threads all made from the cotton plant. The plants grow in warm climates and the fibers, eventually spun into yarn, are attached to the seeds of the fruit, in a boll. To pre-

pare the yarn, the cotton is first freed from the seeds, cleaned, loosened, and carded. Next it's drawn out into slubbing or roving, and is then spun. Depending on the spin and weave, it can be made into the finest muslin or the heaviest canvas.

## COUCHING (HEAVIER THREADS ON TOP OF FABRIC)
Technique in which a thread of any thickness is sewn onto the ground material by means of a different and generally finer thread visible as a pattern. Used when the main thread would be damaged if pulled through the ground material, when it is too thick to pull through, or when it is too expensive to waste by being underneath.

## CRAZY PATCHWORK QUILT
Pieces of fabric of different shapes, types, and colors joined together in a random pattern with no recognizable repeat.

## CREWELWORK
Embroidery made with colored wool yarns stitched on unbleached cotton or linen, usually in a vine or leaf formation, with floral details added. It was very popular in England during the late-17th century and is still used today in decoration.

## CUTWORK
Embroidery on fabric common in the 16th and 17th centuries, which was the forerunner of all the needle-made laces. Part of the ground fabric is cut away, and threads, which are buttonholed over and then joined to each other in pattern, cross the resulting space.

## DALMATIC
Vestment worn by a deacon assisting at the Eucharist and other solemn services. In the 2nd century, it was an overtunic with wide straight sleeves, as worn in Dalmatia, and it was generally decorated with two vertical stripes from shoulder to hem which later developed into the more modern orphrey.

## DAMASK
Originally a rich silk fabric with woven floral designs made in China and introduced to Europe through Damascus, from which it derived its name. Now a broad group of jacquard-woven fabrics with elaborate floral or geometric patterns, made of linen, cotton, wool, worsted, silk, rayon, acetate, and other manufactured fibers, and combinations of these fibers. The pattern is distinguished from the ground by contrasting luster and is reversible. In two-color damask, the colors reverse on either side. The fabric is similar to brocade, but flatter, and reversible.

The pomegranate motif signifying fruitfulness and fertility has been worked in dival stitch embroidery.

The artichoke plant motif, symbolizing peace or hope, is also included in this early 19th century Ottoman empire arabesque, stylized vining line

**DAMASK DARN / DAMASK PATCH**
Darn is used in the repairing of damask woven table linen, where the tear is usually on the cross of the fabric. Two edges of the slit are drawn together, and a first block of darning on the straight of the thread is worked, then the second block, at right angles to the first, is worked. Patching is a method of repairing holes in table linen. A well-washed piece of similar fabric is tacked underneath the hole and the edges of the tear are darned down on the patch, which is then cut away on the wrong side.

**DIRECTOIRE STYLE**
Neo-classical French style, especially in furniture, reflecting the political Directoire period (1795–99), and recognized by austere classical forms, sometimes decorated with revolutionary symbols such as the fasces (a bundle of reeds with an axe head) and the cap of liberty.

**DISSOLUTION OF THE MONASTERIES**
Henry VIII, in 1537, profoundly affected the art of embroidery in England. Since most embroidery was worked for the churches and religious houses, with the Reformation, the advent of Protestantism, and the loss of the monasteries and monastic life, the whole pattern of embroidery changed. Work for the church ceased, so the talents of embroiderers turned exclusively to secular objects.

**DIVAL EMBROIDERY**
Metallic embroidery that does not pierce the ground fabric but lies on top in parallel stitches. A different thread is brought up from underneath the fabric to hold the metal threads around the edges of the design. Padding is used to give the motif a three-dimensional look.

**DOWN**
Finest, softest bird feathers, which have almost no hard center vane. It is the best filling for cushions, eiderdowns, and quilts, and appears in a form of swansdown trimming in the late 18th and 19th centuries.

**DUPIONI**
Silk reeled from a cocoon formed by two worms, producing strands simultaneously or drawn from two cocoons. This yarn has excellent tensile strength.

**EAST INDIA COMPANY**
English company founded in 1600 for the purpose of trade with India, China, and the East. While the main object was to acquire spices for England, embroideries were also both exported and imported.

**ECCLESIASTIC**
Of or associated with a church.

**ECRU**
Word from the French, meaning raw or unbleached, used to denote a pale beige or natural color, especially of lace.

**ELIZABETHAN STYLE**
Age of Elizabeth I produced the finest embroideries ever worked in England. Partly due to the introduction of fine steel needles and the spirit of the Renaissance, the love of finery and rich fabrics of the court and nobility, the emergence of pattern books and aids for the home embroiderer, and the rise in power and wealth of the trading classes. It was characterized by symmetrical façades, arcaded friezes, strap work, grotesques, arabesques, heraldic motifs, and bulbous supports.

**ELYSEE WORK**
Embroidery of the late 19th century in which a running spray of leaves and tendrils is cut out of one fabric and pasted onto another. When dry, stems, veins, and stamens are embroidered.

**EMBOSSED**
An effect obtained by rolling fabric between engraved cylinders so that the design appears in relief on the face of the cloth.

**EMBROIDERY**
The art of ornamenting material with needlework. The basis of embroidery has always been plain sewing, but nowadays more emphasis is put on the decorative qualities of different threads and materials than on the underlying skills and techniques which earlier, and especially before the advent of the sewing machine, were considered essential. Embroidery undoubtedly followed soon after man learned to weave, and in Scandinavia, simply embroidered woolen garments have been found dating from the Bronze Age, while Chinese embroideries of the 5th century BCE can still be seen whose style shows that the craft must have started much earlier in order to have reached such a high level of sophistication by that time. Until the 19th century, there were only a few well-defined techniques, named for their style rather than for the materials on which they were worked. However, by the end of the 19th century, many new names and types had appeared with the development of the art needlework movement, the art needlework departments in stores, and the big firms selling threads, transfers, and materials. In many cases, these new names of embroideries were just old friends freshened up, but their profusion has made for confusion.

**EMPIRE STYLE**
The period of Napoleanic rule lends its name to the late Neoclassical style that

characterizes the artistic creations of the era, including the Directoire and Consulate periods. Napoleon I visited French textile, porcelain, and furniture workshops to encourage their increased production for the greater glory of France, and all the arts served to promote his regime. Revolutionary conquests were echoed in the fine and decorative arts, in which figures of Fame and Victory abounded.

**FELT**
A non-woven cloth of matted layers (usually wool) that are formed into a sheet by means of moisture and pressure.

**FESTOON**
A looped ornament, like a wreath or garland, which consists of themes such as flowers, fruits, leaves, or drapery. Usually ends are punctuated with some form of ornament, such as a lion's head, rosettes, or other classical motifs.

**FIBER**
The basic constituent of textiles. Technically fibers are long-chain molecules; they can be short or long, straight or naturally twisted, soft or hard, depending on their origins and functions within their source. Some fibers can be matted together and spun, like cotton; while others are unwound from their natural forms, as silk from its cocoon.

**FILIGREE**
Fine silver or gold wire twisted to form lace-like decorative openwork.

**FLAX**
Plant *Linum usitatissimum*, from which linen is made. After stalks have been cut, they are laid in bundles in water until the outer fibers have rotted away. This is known as retting. The fine fibers left are then spun and woven into linen. In colonial America, it took 18 months from the planting of the seed to the finished homespun linen.

**FLEUR DE LYS**
"Flower of the lily" is a stylized flower and the royal emblem of France. In Christian theology, it represents the holy trinity.

**FLORENTINE EMBROIDERY**
(BARGELLO WORK, HUNGARIAN POINT, FLAME STITCH)
Form of work using floss silk, the thread employed in some of the embroideries of India and China, some ecclesiastical embroidery, and any household embroidery where the article will not get hard wear and where delicate shading is required.

**FORTUNY**
Mariano Fortuny y Madrazo (May 11, 1871–May 3, 1949), son of the Spanish painter Mariano Fortuny y Marsal, was the creator of rich and lustrous fabrics from Venice, Italy. In the early 1900s Mariano Fortuny developed his own unique method for printing fabrics, based on his years of studying ancient alchemy and dyeing techniques, and his extensive experimentation with different fabrics, dyes, and processes. The production of these textiles was the culmination of his knowledge of engineering, color, design, and art, in one manifestation of pure artistic genius. In 1919, Fortuny moved the production of his textiles from his home to a former convent on the island of Giudecca. It was here that he installed larger versions of the machines he designed and built in order to print his fabrics on a wider raw material. Thanks to the efforts of Fortuny's wife, Henriette, and American interior designer (and his initial distributor), Elsie McNeill, the factory continued operation even after Fortuny's death. Today the historic company is still thriving under the leadership of Maury and Mickey Riad.

**FRANCE**
A country known for producing some of the finest tapestries, woven fabrics (especially silks), clothing, and embroideries. French work is noted for its sense of style and designs, combined with meticulous workmanship, coming from a long tradition of royal patronage.

**FRIZE**
Type of purl formed by winding tinsel onto a square mold. It is then cut into short lengths and sewn on like a bead.

**GALÓN** (GALLOON)
Decorative braid or tape of cotton, silk, gold, or silver threads commonly used in trimming or binding.

**GEORGIAN**
The period in English history between 1714 and 1830, when the four Georges were on the throne.

**GIMP**
A narrow ornamental trim used in sewing or embroidery. It is made of silk, wool, or cotton, and is stiffened with metallic wire or coarse cord running through it.

**GLAZED CHINTZ**
Printed or plain cotton fabric with resin (starch or wax) finish applied by pressure over heated steam rollers, resulting in a polished surface.

**GOLD EMBROIDERY** (See METAL THREAD EMBROIDERY)
Embroidery worked with threads of gold, gilt, silver, aluminum, or copper and metal spangles or sequins, called "gold embroidery," as gold thread is most often used. At one time it was synonymous with ecclesiastical embroidery, although metal threads were used in heraldic work and for badges as well.

**GOTHIC**
Style based on medieval architecture, characterized by pointed and ogee arches, tracery, pinnacles, cusps, crockets, trefoils, and quatrefoils.

**GOUT GREC**
Louis XVI style, from the French "Greek taste," the contemporary term used in France in the 1760s to describe the early Neoclassical style, with emphasis on geometric forms and decoration based on ancient architecture of Greece. Motifs include volutes, bay leaf swags, Vitruvian scrolls, palmettos, and guilloché.

**GREEK KEY**
Pattern based on ancient Greek decoration consisting of repeated interlocking right-angled lines. It was often used in a continuous band in classically inspired ornament.

**GREIGE GOODS**
Plain fabric coming directly off the loom before it has been bleached or finished. Used mainly for printing.

**GRIFFIN**
Motif of a mythical creature with the head and wings of an eagle and the body of a lion, typically depicted with pointed ears and with eagle's legs replacing the forelegs.

**GRISAILLE BEADWORK**
Monochromatic beadwork designs on a ground of Berlin woolwork. Black, grey, white (both clear and opaque), and steel beads are used. Very popular in the mid-19th century and was made up into articles such as banner fire screens, mantel covers, and tea cosies.

**GROS POINT**
A non-directional pile fabric that is warp-looped. It is hard-wearing and extremely resilient. Made of wool or synthetic fibers, it has larger loops than a frieze and resembles the ground area of needlepoint.

**GROTESQUE**
An elaborate type of ornament consisting of linked human figures, animals, mythical beasts, or birds among intertwining scrolls and foliage, often in vertical structure incorporating candelabra forms. The decoration was first popular during the Renaissance.

**GROUND**
Background area of a pattern. Also used to describe the base fabric on which embroidery or appliqué is stitched.

**GUARDED**
Term meaning edged with lace, braid, or embroidery, frequently used in 15th and 16th centuries.

**GUILLOCHÉ**
A pattern of continuous twisting bands forming interlacing circles, sometimes enclosing rosettes or other motifs, and derived from classical architecture. This ornament was revived in the Renaissance and was widespread in the Neoclassical period.

**GUIMPED EMBROIDERY**
Type of embroidery where the pattern must be drawn on the material and the figures of the pattern also cut in parchment, vellum, or cloth, over which the gold or silver is sewn with a fine silk thread. This method of slightly raising or padding goldwork is considered one of the techniques used in metal thread embroidery, rather than a type of embroidery on its own.

**GUIPURE WORK**
Indefinite term with a variety of meanings, including lace with a raised thread, darned net or filet, a form of embroidery in which almost all the ground material was cut away, leaving the parts of the pattern joined together only by narrow bars. The word comes from "guiper" in French, meaning to cover a thread with silk.

**HAWAIIAN QUILTS**
Patchwork quilts made in Hawaii. These differ from the more usual American quilt in that they are always made of new material, in two colors only, and the design consists of one motif repeated four times, which is cut out and applied to the ground fabric.

**HERALDIC EMBROIDERY**
Representation of coats of arms, crests, and insignia on textiles.

**HOMESPUN**
Fabric made from yarn spun at home, either wool or linen, and so by inference rather coarse, plain, and of uneven texture.

**HUGUENOTS** (FRENCH PROTESTANTS SPECIALIZED IN TEXTILES)
French Protestants fled after the revocation of the Edict of Nantes, which had allowed freedom of worship in 1685.

Huguenot refugees were highly skilled craftsmen, and influential in other countries, such as Britain, especially in silversmithing and textiles.

**HUMERAL VEIL**
Long oblong vestment of silk worn around the shoulders of Roman Catholic priests to envelop their hands when carrying the sacred vessels. It should be light enough to drape well and can be decorated with embroidery.

**ICONOGRAPHY**
Representation of a person or object by any form of design. Often refers to saints and prophets, where they are shown with the objects that have become associated with them, such as the keys of St. Peter or the gridiron of Saint Lawrence.

**IKAT**
A resist-dyeing technique in which yarns are tie-dyed before they are woven into cloth. The term derives from Indonesian "mengikat" meaning "to tie" or "to bind."

**INCRUST**
To ornament a surface with a layer or crust of another material, most commonly jewels, gold cord, or braid and lace, the latter being very common in the late 19th and early 20th centuries.

**INDIAN EMBROIDERY**
The modern history of India started with the founding of the Mughal Dynasty in 1526. Although of central Asian origin, the Mughals had assimilated the culture of Persia, and Emperor Akbar (1542), keenly interested in the arts, brought Persian craftsman to India where they worked with the natives in workshops. The result was a blend of two cultures that has remained the dominant characteristic of Indian embroidery. Typified by the use of chain stitch worked with a hook called an ari, metal threads, mirror glass or shisha mirror, beetle wings, and exquisite work on very fine muslins.

**INDIENNES**
Floral embroidered and printed cottons from India popular in 17th century France and England, which continued to influence European textile design in the 18th. Flowers with stylized patterning in the petal and splaying fern-like leaves were typical elements.

**INDIGO**
A blue dye whose color compound, indigotin, is found in leaves of tropical and subtropical plants of the genus Indigofera. Indigo-bearing plants are found naturally in India, Africa, and the Americas. Indigo blue is best known as the dye of denim for blue jeans.

**INDO EUROPEAN EMBROIDERY**
Embroidery that came to England from India in the 17th century and was thought for many years to be truly Indian. However, Irwin (1959, keeper of the Indian Sections at the Victoria and Albert Museum in London) has shown conclusively from the records of the East India Company that this work was embroidered from designs and suggestions sent to India from England and worked by the Indian in his own idiom.

**INDO-PORTUGUESE EMBROIDERY**
An adapted style of Portuguese European embroidery that developed in India after the Portuguese infiltration, beginning in 1501. The Portuguese Jesuit missionaries set up schools and brought with them illustrated books, religious vestments, and church furnishings. This inspired new design motifs of Old Testament themes, European hunters, and classical Greco-Roman legends, which combine with the traditional Hindu mythological heroes, animals, and decorative motifs.

**ITALIAN CUTWORK** (See RETICELLE)
An Italian needlepoint technique, which is on the border between embroidery and lace. It is one of the cutwork variations of 15th, 16th, and 17th centuries, coming from Venice. The earliest work was made with a basis of fabric from which most of the threads were drawn or cut, forming squares. These were buttonholed around and then crossed with threads in patterns that were also buttonholed.

**JACQUARD**
A system of weaving that, because of a pattern-making mechanism of great versatility, permits the production of woven designs of considerable size. The jacquard loom was invented by Joseph Marie Jacquard in the early 19th century. In this system of weaving, the weave pattern is copied from the design paper by punching a series of cards, each perforation controlling the action of one warp end, for the passage of one pick. Depending upon the design, the machine may carry a large number of cards because there is a separate card for each pick.

## KAFTAN
See CAFTAN

## KANTHAS
Quilted coverlets and shawls made entirely from waste fabrics, by the women of Bengal. Running stitches that form the quilting are worked in plain or whirling patterns of flowers, animals, and scenes of domestic life. When finished, extra medallions are embroidered on top.

## KILIM
Tapestry-woven rug without a pile, with clear colors and bold patterns.

## KIMONO
Long robe with loose sleeves, fastened with a sash or obi, and woven in Japan. Often beautifully and lavishly embroidered, especially for ceremonial occasions.

## KUBA TEXTILES
Woven from a raffia palm leaf fiber in the Democratic Republic of the Congo (formerly Zaïre), these geometrical patterned cloths are usually rectangular or square. The cloth is very coarse when first cut from the loom, so it is pummeled with a mortar to soften it.

## LAIDWORK
Laying down of a foundation of long threads, which are then tied down in pattern by other threads crossing them. This type of embroidery has been popular at various times in most parts of the world, and different countries have interpreted the basic definition in different ways. There are three distinct varieties: Solid—where the ground threads are placed touching another—found in parts of the Bayeux Tapestry and in various pieces of Opus Anglicanum; Open—where the threads are laid at intervals, with crossing threads laid at the same interval to form open squares, which are then tied down at the corners. This kind can often be seen in English crewelwork hangings of the 17th century; and Oriental—another form of couching, where the same thread both lays and ties, as in the medieval white embroideries from Germany and Switzerland.

## LAMÉ
Originally a very thin, gilded or plated sheet of metal that can be cut into shapes or strips with scissors or a punch, and which is much used in In-

dian embroidery for decorating net, muslin, and other suitable fabrics. The name is also currently given to a variety of fabrics woven from metallic thread.

## LAMBREKIN
A short, decorative drapery for a shelf edge or for the top of a window casing. See VALENCE. Also a term describing a scarf used to cover a knight's helmet in the middle ages.

## LAMPAS
A compound weave used to produce luxurious silks, often with a surface of gold or silver thread. The structure is created from a warp-faced weave for the ground and a weft-faced weave for the pattern.

## LINEN
Cloth woven from the fibers of flax. It has the longest known history of any fabric and probably originated with the Egyptians. It is very cool to the touch and wrinkles easily.

## LOUIS XIV (1643-1715)
Architectural and decorative arts style fashionable in France during Louis XIV's reign, emphasizing grandeur, symmetry, formality, and luxury, using motifs inspired by classical art. He was known as the Sun King.

## LOUIS XV (1715-1774)
Architectural and decorative arts style fashionable to France during Louis XV's reign, including the Régence period (1715-1723) when the king was a minor, characterized by smaller, lighter forms, with naturalistic motifs such as shells and rockwork, and progressing to the full-blown Rococo style.

## LOUIS XVI (1774-1793)
Architectural and decorative arts style fashionable in France during Louis XVI's reign, which was both the last of the Rococo and the first of Neoclassicism.

## MACHINE EMBROIDERY
(free embroidery, freehand embroidery, art embroidery, free-motion embroidery, flat embroidery) Work done either on a domestic sewing machine or on a trade machine designed for embroidery. The first hand embroidery machine was invented by Josué Heilman of Mulhouse (France) in 1828. At the Great Exhibition of 1851, Houldsworth & Company displayed examples of patent machine embroideries, polychrome on various fabrics. Switzerland was known for fine cotton embroidery on muslin, and there the new machines were used to develop

this kind of work. Soon the quality was high enough to compete with hand embroidery. By the 1850s and 1860s, the industry had become very prosperous. By the 1870s, women's dresses were loaded with trimming of every kind. By the 1920s and 1930s, the idea of creative embroidery by machine was born (until then, it was used only for household and repetitive dress designs).

## MADEIRA WORK
Development from broderie anglaise, which was so popular in the mid-19th century for trimming dresses and underwear. The technique emigrated with nuns to Madeira, an island off the northwest coast of Africa, where it was taught to the peasant women and has become one of the major exports and tourist buys of the island. In addition to the plain overcast holes and buttonholed edges of broderie anglaise, Madeira work has a small amount of surface embroidery, meticulously worked.

## MANIPLE
A strip of fabric embroidered en suite with the stole, which is worn over the left forearm of a priest, deacon, or subdeacon at the celebration of the Eucharist in the Western Church. The maniple symbolizes the towel used by Christ when washing the feet of the disciples.

## MANNERIST STYLE
From the Italian "maniera," meaning virtuosity or sophistication, it was the late Renaissance decorative style developed in the 16th century, making much use of perspective and attenuated forms, and incorporating exaggerated, twisted, and fantastical animals, sea creatures, and birds ensnared by grotesques and strapwork. This type of improvisation on classical conventions was seen at its most highly developed in Florence and Fountainbleau. The style evolved into Auricular, and led to the Baroque.

## MANTLE
An outer garment like a cloak worn at different periods by men, women, and children, with slight variations in shape. Also referred to as the outer garment worn by the sovereign and peers at a coronation, or the garment worn by women in the last quarter of the 19th century. The beautifully and richly decorated covering for the Scroll or Sefer Torah, most sacred object of the Jewish faith. Mantles are generally professional work of the highest standard, using rich fabrics and metal threads, cords, and purls.

## MATELASSE
A double-woven cloth, using two sets of warp and filler threads for an embossed pattern in one color that simulates a quilted effect.

## MEANDER
In textiles, a wave-like pattern.

## MEDIEVAL
A term referring to the Middle Ages in Europe that spans from about AD 500 to ACE 1500, but the exact dates are widely debated. Historians argue a variety of events that date the Middle Ages as roughly the period after the fall of Rome to the events leading to the modern world, such as the discovery of America in 1492, or the Reformation in 1517. Generally speaking it is the time between the ancient periods to the birth of the modern ages.

## MERCERIZED
A high-quality finishing process of cotton yarn in which the application of caustic soda and tension develops a smooth, lustrous surface.

## METAL THREAD EMBROIDERY
Embroidery worked with threads of gold, gilt, silver, aluminum, or copper, and metal spangles or sequins, and sometimes called gold embroidery, as gold thread is most often used. Similar to ecclesiastical embroidery, because metal threads were used in heraldic work and for badges, also. See GUIMPED EMBROIDERY.

## METALLIC YARN
Thin sheets of pure metal—gold, silver, gilt silver, or copper—cut into strips and used as flat elements. The majority of metallic yarns are composed of a very fine metal leaf adhered to a substrate, called a lamella, made of paper, leather, animal gut, or membrane. These metal-leafed lamellae can then be used in textiles, either as flat strips or wound around a core yarn. The yarns are used for embroidery and weaving.

## MODERNISM
Inspired by a need to escape from past excessive decoration, this style of the early 20th century embraced machine technology and favored geometric forms and smooth, uncluttered surfaces.

## MOHAIR
A wool-like fiber derived from the fleece of the Angora goat. It is renowned for its luxurious, soft quality, yet extremely hard-wearing characteristic.

## MOIRE
Fabric with a "watered mark" motif, which is achieved by application of intense but uneven pressure from heated cylinders to a folded, dampened rep (fabric) cloth. The crushing process creates the irregular pattern.

## MOLLUSK
A shellfish, the source of purple dye in ancient South and Central America, and still used in Guatemala in the mid-20th century. Thread is dyed in the saliva

A brown heavy silk thread is couched with a tinier brown thread to provide an outline.

The thickly padded trapunto work gives this textile its sculptural look.

A dark-gold metallic galon is hand-stitched over the embroidery.

produced by rubbing the mollusks together, creating purple dye.

**MONK'S CLOTH**
Heavy, coarse cotton fabric loosely woven in 2x2- to 8x8-thread basket weaves and often used as a ground for embroidery. In America it is known as abbot's cloth, belfry cloth, and druid's cloth.

**MORESQUE DECORATION**
See ARABESQUE

**MORSE**
The clasp that fastens a cope. Usually jeweled or enameled, sometimes embroidered, in which case any fine, flat stitching is usually protected by raised metal threads or braids.

**MOSS WORK**
Type of 16th- and 17th-century embroidery, which had not been identified, though from its name it would appear to consist of French knots close together, or perhaps the dyed purl thread that is so often found in embroidery of that time.

**MOTIF**
A distinctive part of a design that can be isolated as a unit, appearing only once, repeated, or varied.

**MUGHALS** (MOGULS)
A race of Central Asian origin that conquered India in 1526 and ruled there until after the Indian Mutiny of 1857-1858. Their emperors, especially Akbar (1542-1605), encouraged the arts, including embroidery.

**NAP**
Raised surface of cloth or carpets made by one of three methods—1. Teasing up the smooth surface with an instrument such as the head of a teasel plant or with machinery. 2. Weaving in raised loops, which are subsequently cut and smoothed, as in velvet. 3. Making loops by hand on canvas, as in plush stitch or surrey stitch, which are then cut and sheared to the requisite depth.

**NATURAL FIBER**
Any textile fiber manufactured from an animal or vegetable source. Cotton, linen, silk, and wool are the foremost examples.

**NEEDLEPOINT**
Hand embroidery that is stitched through a stiff open-weave canvas, typically in a diagonal stitch often referred to as the tent stitch, and covering the entire surface of the canvas fabric. The smallest version of this is called petit point.

**NEOCLASSICISM**
Style based on the forms and ornamentation of ancient Greece and Rome, which lasted with variations in emphasis from 1760-1830.

**NUÉ**
French term meaning shaded or cloudy, used to refer to silk yarns colored in different shades along a single yarn.

**NIMBUS**
Elaborate type of halo which in art surrounds the head of Christ, God, the Virgin Mary, and sometimes the Evangelists and Apostles. Usually takes the form of a halo, divided by a cruciform cross. It is rendered in gold work on many ecclesiastical embroideries.

**NUN'S CLOTH**
Woollen tabby-woven fabric used as a dress material in the mid-18th century, and because of its even weave and many colors, as a ground for embroidery. In America, this is known as bunting.

**OGEE**
A shallow, S-shaped curve found in a moulding profile; also used to form a Gothic-style pointed arch with reversed curves on either side of the apex.

**OMBRE**
A fabric made by laying in wefts of yarn that are closely colored hues that, after weaving, create a graduated, shaded effect. Origin: French, *ombre*—shadow.

**OR NUÉ**
Literally means, "shaded gold." A type of couching in which gold threads are laid horizontally, generally on a plain woven linen foundation, and held in place with polychrome silk threads, producing a shaded effect.

**ORPHREY**
A word derived from the Latin *auriphrygium*, meaning gold embroidery. It now refers to bands of embroidery, often of gold or silk thread, on the front edges of copes, the back of chasubles, and on some altar frontals.

**PADDING**
Material sometimes called wadding used as the interlining for quilting or the filling for flat cushions. Material is generally string felt or card, used to build up

all types of padded embroidery, especially goldwork.

**PAILLETTE** (See SPANGLE)
Small flat ornament used to add brilliance and glitter to fabric and embroideries. Usually shiny metal (gold, silver, brass, or copper) and have a hole for sewing them down. Also known as sequin.

**PAISLEY**
A distinctive, intricate pattern of curved, feather-shaped figures based on a pine cone or *boteh* design that originated in India.

**PALLADIAN STYLE**
Inspired by the 16th-century work of Italian architect Andrea Palladio (1508-1580), it is a classical style of European architecture of the first half of the 18th century, which particularly affected furniture in England. The style is recognizable by its solid symmetrical forms and pediments, columns, and scrolled brackets, and decorated with acanthus, swags, masks, lion paws, and other forms derived from classical architecture.

**PALMETTE**
A classical ornamental motif derived from a stylized palm leaf, closely resembling the anthemion, and much used in the Neoclassical period.

**PARCHMENT**
Dressed skin of sheep, goat, or other animals prepared for use as a writing material before the introduction of paper. Parchment being fairly stiff, embroiderers used it for padding goldwork, and also to back cutwork while it was being worked, after which, the parchment would be removed. Vellum is better-quality parchment.

**PASSEMENTERIE**
Elaborately constructed, braided and corded trimmings and tassels, gimps, edge-bindings, and cords that are used to embellish curtains, upholstery, pillows, and other furnishings. The name is derived from the French "passement," to braid.

**PELISSE**
Full-length cloak, often made of silks or lightweight fabrics, and decorated with rouleaux or embroidery, which were worn by women in the late-18th and early-19th centuries. Often lined with fur.

**PENELOPE CANVAS** (DUO CANVAS)
First canvas to be woven with double, instead of single, threads. Invented in the 1830s and called Penelope—after the wife of Ulysses, who spent her nights unpicking the work she had done during the day—the two-thread canvas looked to needle workers (who

had been used to only single thread) as though the work had been unpicked. It rapidly became and is still a very popular medium for fairly heavyweight work, especially since it is possible to spare the threads and do both coarse and fine work on the same canvas.

**PENTALPHA**
Five-pointed star often used as a symbol in ecclesiastical embroidery.

**PERSIAN EMBROIDERY**
Persia (now called Iran), in a direct line of the silk road from East to West, has always been famous for textiles, and even more for design. As a predominantly Moslem country, the representation of living creatures is rare, formal pattern and stylized figures taking its place. When the Mughals conquered north India, the Emperor Akbar brought Persian embroiderers in to work with the Indians, and much Indian design shows this combination of talent. Over the centuries, three main motifs emerged that appear to us as typical; Tree of Life, which evolved into a stylized splay of flowers; the cypress tree, with its narrow, upright shape; and the carnation, stylized or naturalistic, all used over and over again. Stitches generally used are double darning, chain, stem, and long and short.

**PHULKARI** (INDIAN EMBROIDERY)
Flowered work. It is embroidery worked by the women of the Punjab for head veils and other garment pieces.

**PICOT**
Small loop of twisted thread, generally but not always forming an edging to lace or embroidery. It can also mean a raised loop or bead representing organic things such as a grain of corn or the vein of a leaf.

**PINKING**
The ornamentation of material by cutting or punching different shapes in it; also the decoration of a raw edge by punching out a zigzag pattern on it, which also has the effect of preventing fraying.

**PIPING**
A strip of fabric, usually cut on the bias, which may or may not enclose a thin cord. It is inserted into a plain seam to form decorative trimming.

**PIQUE EMBROIDERY**
Embroidery that has a cord outlining the main part of the design, with filling stitches imitating a figured fabric. This type of work was popular in the 19th century, and was used extensively on children's clothes and certain household articles.

## PLATE
A strip of metal, generally gilt, which is flat, bright, and shining, and is used in ecclesiastical and metal-thread embroidery. Usually couched down with a matching or contrasting thread either in a straight line or folded, so that the couching thread does not show.

## PLY
Threads or yarns twisted together for strength; usually bought in 1-, 2-, 3-, or 4-ply thicknesses.

## POLISHED COTTON
A combed and carded fabric in satin construction, which has been calendered to lend a high luster to the surface.

## POLYCHROME
Term describing the use of several colors in a piece of work.

## PORTIÈRE
Curtain hung over a door, doorway, or arch to give privacy, to exclude drafts, or for decoration. As they are big and flat, they lend themselves to large scale, so embroidery was often applied. They were used in medieval houses and were popular in the interior decoration of the late-19th and early-20th centuries.

## PUNTO
Italian word for stitch, and used the same way as the French word *point*. It means a stitch made in needlepoint lace, but in various forms of cutwork, which were the antecedents of lace, punto is used with another word to describe early techniques; for example, *punto tagliato* (cutwork), *punto tirato* (drawn threadwork), and *punto in aria* (needlepoint lace).

## PURLED
Cord sewn down with widely spaced buttonhole stitch, and used as an edging for applied work in America. Thread for stitching can be silk, cotton, or chenille.

## QUATREFOIL
A four-lobe shape seen in Gothic style. The term generally refers in embroidery to a four-petal flower or to the architectural detail sometimes found in opus anglicanum, where an arch or opening is so shaped as to give the appearance of a four-petal flower.

## QUEEN ANNE STYLE
The restrained form of the Baroque classical style seen in domestic design during the early 18th century, and revived as part of the Aesthetic Movement in the late 19th century.

## QUILTING
Stitching together of two or three thicknesses of fabric to make something warm, protective, or decorative.

## RAISED
Term applied to fabric partly woven with a pile so that some of it appears to have been cut away, leaving the other part raised. It applies to all embroidery that is not flat but is worked in relief by means of card, parchment, string, cotton, wool, padding, or just by the use of thick thread.

## RAISED EMBROIDERY
Type of embroidery often consisting of flowers and buds worked in satin stitch over a pad of cotton wool which was carefully cut to shape and fastened to the ground fabric with a large cross stitch. Next, satin stitch in embroidery cotton was worked over the pad; and finally, satin stitch in the appropriate thread and colors.

## RAFFIA
Soft fibers from the leaves of the raffia from Madagascar used for embroidery in many African countries, the Caribbean islands, as well as Britain and the United States. Kuba cloth is made from raffia.

## RAFFIA EMBROIDERY
Embroidery using raffia as the thread, suitable for coarse work on raffia cloth, canvas, crash, or hessian. Kuba, Bakuba, and Kasai tribes in Africa use such techniques as over-sewing, open-work, eyelet, or buttonhole-stitched—and embroidered pile cloth. Raffia can be dyed bright colors, and so, lends itself to decoration on garden hats and aprons, and workbags. As it is comparatively cheap and covers the ground quickly, raffia has always been one of the threads used in teaching embroidery to children.

## RAW SILK
Silk reeled off from the cocoon but not yet spun and woven. There are three kinds: floss, organzine, and tram. It is in this state that the silk is bought by a manufacturer.

## REGENCE
The French style of circa 1720-1730, during the regency of Philippe, Duc D'Orléans (1715-1723), for the young Louis XV style and early period of Rococo.

## REGENCY
Referring to the period in British history from 1811-1820 when George, Prince of Wales, acted as Regent for his father, George III. In the arts it was generally accepted as an extension of Neoclassicism, when all things Greek and Roman were particularly admired, and embroidery followed the same lines, with the use of classical motifs.

## RENAISSANCE
From the Italian, meaning "rebirth," it was the cultural revival of classical Greek and Roman art ideas that began in Florence in the 14th century, and eventually spread throughout Europe. The style is based on symmetrical architectural and sculptural forms with classical motifs such as trophies, acanthus leaves, and human and mythological creatures and grotesques.

## REP
A ribbed fabric that is woven in very fine cords or ribs across the width of the piece and usually of cotton, silk, or wool.

## REPEAT
A continuous pattern designed so that the pattern along the edges on a section of fabric or wallpaper will match up with the pattern on a neighboring section, allowing the pattern to continue seamlessly.

## RESHT WORK
A type of patchwork or appliqué where small pieces of flannel wool are sewn to a foundation of cotton or wool by decorative buttonhole, chain, and feather stitches. Originating in Resht, Iran, the technique is centuries old but still produced today.

## RESIST PRINTING
A general term for printing with a dye-resistant substance, leaving only the background color after a washed finish. Its origins date to the 18th century when a resist paste was used to inhibit indigo dye.

## RESTORATION STYLE
A decorative-arts style linked to the reign of Charles II (1660-1685), after his restoration to the throne. In contrast to the austere Commonwealth era, it reflected a taste for opulence, with French, Dutch, and Portuguese influences. Embroideries usually described by this name are large crewelwork hangings, tent-stitch pictures, and raised or stumpwork.

## RETICULATION
A net or web-like pattern created by lozenge-shaped, pierced, interlaced, or interwoven decoration.

## RIBBON WORK OR RIBBON APPLIQUÉ
In decorative design, a motif largely composed of ribbons—tied in knots, festooned or flowing—often used in the Italian Renaissance. A type of embroidery that was popular in the 1870s, in which narrow silk ribbon was gathered up and formed into petals, the edges of leaves, and the insides of buds, and sewn onto cloth, with embroidery stitches completing the design. The ribbon had a silky, crinkly look highly applicable to flowers such as poppies.

## RICHELIEU EMBROIDERY
Type of whitework where, as in Renaissance embroidery, the design is outlined in buttonhole stitch, the fabric cut away, and the spaces joined with bars or brides. The difference between the two types is that here, the joining bars are decorated with picots.

## RINCEAU
A French term that describes a continuous scrolling motif, usually consisting of acanthus or vining leaves. Used in carved, molded, and plastered Neoclassical decoration as well as in embroidery.

## ROCAILLES
An 18th-century artistic or architectural style of decoration characterized by elaborate ornamentation with pebbles and shells, typical of grottos and fountains.

## ROCOCO
The style that evolved from a lightening of Baroque formality in early-18th century France, to embrace more naturalistic and non-classical decoration. It is characterized by asymmetry, scrollwork, exoticism (for example, chinoiserie), rocailles, and pale color. It affected the decorative arts in all of Europe and the United States until at least the 1770s.

## ROLLER PRINTING
Sometimes referred to as cylinder- or machine printed, this technique was first developed in 1783. Engraved rollers apply the design to fabric as it passes between metal cylinders.

## ROMANESQUE
Architectural style of Romanized Europe between the Classical and Gothic periods, especially evident in some French cathedrals. The term is used in embroidery when describing designs based on this form of architecture.

## ROSETTE
Term meaning "like a rose" and found in needlework in almost every culture and most periods. It is a form that looks like a rose.

## SACRED MONOGRAM
The letters IHS stand for the first three letters of the name Jesus in Greek, IESOUS. Iota (I) and Eta (H) and

Sigma (S). This monogram is found frequently in ecclesiastical embroidery.

**SARI**
Length of fabric worn as the main garment by Hindu women. Draped around the body, with one end thrown over the head or shoulder. Saris may be printed cotton, printed or beautifully embroidered silk, or man-made fibers; they have a narrow border at the sides and a deep border at the bottom end.

**SATIN**
A weave rather than a fabric. Satin is twilled but over an irregular number of warp threads, so that the surface weft threads entirely hide the warp, producing a smooth surface that is afterwards calendared and made glossy. Originally from China and made from silk, but may also be made of wool, cotton, a mixture of wool and cotton or synthetics.

**SCREEN PRINTING**
Hand- or machine-table printing process in which a stenciled screen held in a frame is positioned on the cloth and color is applied with a squeegee. Separate screens are required for each color of the pattern.

**SCRIM**
Fine, open-weave canvas of a pleasant brown shade, originally made of low-grade linen, but now of cotton or a blend. The best kind, used for needlework, was imported from Russia. Because of its open weave, scrim is very suitable for work done by the counted thread, and it is attractive enough in itself for the background to be left plain, if necessary.

**SELVAGE**
The lengthwise edges of a piece of cloth, often in a different weave, of heavier threads, and intended to prevent raveling.

**SEAL OF SOLOMON OR STAR OF DAVID**
Two equilateral triangles superimposed to form a six-pointed star, representing perfect God and perfect Man.

**SEQUIN**
See PAILLETTE

**SERPENTINE**
An undulating, curved form seen on case furniture, tables, and chairs, especially of the Rococo period. Wavy metallic galón is described as serpentine.

**SHISHA**
Mirror glass or mica applied to cloth with embroidery stitches. It is a technique practiced in areas of India and Pakistan. Because the mirror glass or mica has no holes with which to sew it

down, it must be held by a criss-cross of threads using an interlacing stitch.

**SHUTTLE**
A thread holder, either the tool on which thread is wound, as in a tatting or knotting shuttle, or a boat-shaped container that holds thread already wound on a bobbin, as in weaving or in a sewing machine.

**SILK**
The fiber produced by the larvae of certain bombycine moths that feed on mulberry leaves. It was the Chinese in about 700 BCE who first managed to rear silkworms and draw off their silk. The secret was so cautiously guarded that it was not until the 6th century ACE that two monks were able to bring some eggs to Europe. From those eggs, sericulture spread to Sicily, Italy, France and Spain, and they became the principal silk centers of southern Europe. The best silk, Tussah or wild-grown, is reeled in Japan, northern China, and India. The beauty of silk thread lies in its lustre and suppleness. It should have as little twist as possible, so that the light reflecting from it can be given full value. The best-quality silk used for producing first-class threads and fabrics is known as net silk, and the waste from this manufacture becomes second quality, called spun silk. The thread takes dye perfectly and can be woven into many different fabrics such as brocade, velvet, satin, and crêpe de Chine.

**SIZE**
Gum-like fluid used for stiffening cloth and to strengthen warp threads in a loom before weaving.

**SOUTACHE**
A narrow, flat, ornamental braid that can be metallic, silk, cotton, or other threads. Usually a soutache has a herringbone weave and is created by two threads being woven over a cord from each side in a methodical right and left motion. It has been called a French herringbone pattern and was often used to decorate military uniforms. It is flatter in appearance than a cording.

**SPAIN**
For the 800 years before 1492, the Moors dominated Spain. After their expulsion, she conquered parts of South America and Mexico. The result is that many of the designs in Spanish work are clearly derived from Arabic modes and, through the Arabs, Persian sources, to which are grafted on elements from Aztec and Inca art. Spain has always been very religious country, so there are many Christian symbols in the folk embroidery, as well as superb ecclesiastical work such as altar frontals, copes, and chasubles.

**SPANGLE**
See PAILLETTE, SEQUIN

**STAMPED VELVET WORK**
Embroidery that merely consists of outlining the pattern on embossed or stamped velvet with silk or metallic thread, to give it greater prominence.

**STITCHERY**
Term for any handwork done with a needle and thread in which a given effect is created. This includes dressmaking, plain sewing, and embroidery. Shakespeare coined the word "stitchery."

**STITCH, TYPES OF**

BARGELLO (FLAME STITCH, FLORENTINE STITCH, HUNGARIAN POINT) Straight stitch, worked in a high- and low-relief pattern forming a zigzag design.

BASKETWEAVE (DIAGONAL TENT STITCH) Tabby weave, but using two or more threads as one, to give a basket-like effect. Basketweave fabric is used for certain types of embroidery. In America, basketweave is the term for the diagonal tent stitch.

BRIAR STITCH (FEATHER STITCH, CAT STITCH, SINGLE CORAL STITCH) The basic stitch of a large group of looped stitches. It is a line stitch and worked by making a blanket stitch alternately either side of a line, in each case, the needle coming out on the line.

BRICK STITCH (LONG AND SHORT STITCH) Only the first row of stitches is in fact alternately long and short; the others are all the same length and fit into the first row, creating a pattern that looks like a brick wall. It is frequently used in shading the petals of flowers.

BURDEN STITCH Couch stitches used in the past and rediscovered by Elizabeth Burden. Rounded, slightly thick threads are laid across the design, leaving a space between each. They are tied down by a stitch crossing two threads, leaving a space, crossing two threads, and so on, with the next row filling the gaps.

CHAIN STITCH (LINE STITCH, FILLING STITCH, OR CANVAS STITCH) One of the oldest and most universal of all stitches, which can be used as a line stitch, filling stitch, or on canvas. Forms interlocking flat chains, and lends itself to a very large number of variations. An embroidery or crochet stitch that forms connecting links like a chain. This can also be a machine stitch. Some suzani designs are created with this stitch, by both hand and machine.

CHINESE KNOT Stitch resembling French knot, often mistaken for them, but flatter, shapelier, and not so

twisted. Seldom used as an isolated stitch, but generally massed together, covering large areas.

CONTINENTAL STITCH (TENT STITCH, CANVAS STITCH, CUSHION STITCH, HALF-CROSS STITCH, NEEDLEPOINT STITCH, PETIT POINT) One of the most widely used counted-thread stitches, dating from the 16th century and earlier. Frequently worked in Tudor households and professional workshops for the pictorial table carpets and hangings that often replaced the earlier tapestries, and later was worked on the finest possible scrim to make panels and pictures as well as upholstered chairs and sofas. Tent stitch can be worked in either horizontal rows, each stitch taken diagonally over on thread, or in diagonal rows (basketweave stitch, in the United States), which has the merit of not distorting the ground fabric and also of making a strongly woven back.

COUCHING A method of embroidering in which a design is made by various threads or cords laid upon the surface of a material and secured by fine stitches drawn through the material from underneath and across the cord to hold it in place on top of the ground.

CONVENT STITCH (COUCHING STITCH, KLOSTER STITCH) Basic stitch in couching, which has been traced back to Scythian embroideries of the 1st century BCE. One thread is laid along the top of the work and is held down by another thread crossing it regularly at right angles or obliquely. Used to outline designs or as filling stitches, and much used in German and Swiss embroideries worked in the convents from the 15th to 17th centuries.

CORAL STITCH Knotted stitch, which can be used for edgings, lines or veining. It changes its shape slightly according to the angle of the needle when crossing the main thread.

CREWEL STITCH (STEM STITCH, OUTLINE STITCH, STALK STITCH, SOUTH KENSINGTON STITCH) One of the most frequently used outline stitches. A long backstitch is taken with the needle coming out halfway along and just beside the stitch, and this is repeated. It is important that the thread always be kept to the same side of the needle. Stem stitch is called crewel stitch because it was the stitch most commonly employed in the 17th century crewel embroideries.

CROSS STITCH (GROS POINT, SAMPLER STITCH) One of the oldest decorative stitches in the world, and used by every ethnic group in some way or other. Worked diagonally from left to right, and crossed back diagonally from right to left.

DARNED EMBROIDERY / "DARNING" Darn—repair in a fabric made by filling the hole with the appropriate thread. Parallel threads are laid across the hole and cross threads are woven alternately over and under. Embroidery—darning is one of the simplest embroidery stitches, and in one form or another many countries have used it at different periods—sometimes as the main stitch but also working as the background stitch. India has always made a specialty of darning, as has Portugal and a number of countries in Eastern Europe. In England it was very popular in the 18th century, and had a revival in a different form in the late 19th, when designs of flowers and leaves were outlined and the ground filled in with darning stitches.

FEATHERSTITCH (BRIAR STITCH, SINGLE CORAL STITCH) Basic stitch of a large group of looped stitches. It is a line stitch, and is worked by making a blanket stitch alternately on either side of a line, in each case, the needle coming out on the line.

FILLING STITCHES Group of stitches used either singly or together to fill a space. Often the same stitches can be adapted as drawn fabric stitches. There are two groups—Single stitches: dot, ermine filling, fly filling, sheaf filling, star filling and ground-cover stitches: darning and variations; Damask darning, pattern darning, diamond filling, honeycomb filling, open-buttonhole filling and variations, fancy-buttonhole filling, paced-buttonhole filling, plaid filling, trellis couching, wave filling.

FLAT STITCHES The group used as outline or filling stitches, which have a flat appearance, though they may be interlaced in working. Stitches include: Algerian eye (star eyelet), arrowhead, basket, basket filling, Bosnian (zigzag), brick, burden, cable outline, chevron, darning and variation, double darning (pesante), dot (rice grain, seeding, single seed, speckling), eyelet, fern, fishbone and variations, open fishbone, overlapping herringbone, raised fishbone, flat (Croatian flat), herringbone and variations, closed, double, Japanese leaf, long

and short (brick embroidery), feather, half-work, Irish, plumage, opus plumarium, shading, surface, tapestry shading, Persian, Portuguese stem, satin and variation, sham satin, straight, stem (stalk Kensington) and variations, crewel (outline), cable stem, and zigzag.

FRENCH KNOT (FRENCH DOT, KNOTTED STITCH, TWISTED KNOT STITCH, WOUND STITCH) Useful stitch consisting of small, isolated knots, which can also be closely grouped. Frequently used to represent the center of flowers. Needle is brought up, the thread is twisted twice around it—holding it taut—and the needle is taken back into the fabric as close as possible to where it emerged.

GOBELIN STITCH The stitch is worked diagonally over two threads in height and one wide, with many variations. This counted thread stitch was invented to imitate woven tapestry. Since the Berlin patterns were based on a square mesh, they were distorted by the technique and the old method of drawing the design directly onto the canvas had to be used.

GROS POINT Cross Stitch. The term is often misapplied to canvas work done with a large tent stitch, and sometimes even used for the whole piece of work as "my gros point." This non-directional pile fabric is warp-looped. It is hard-wearing and extremely resilient. Made of wool or synthetic fibers, it has larger loops than a frieze, and resembles the ground area of needlepoint.

HUNGARIAN STITCH (FLORENTINE STITCH) One of the grounding stitches used in work done by the counted thread, either in fine canvas work and needlepoint for stools, hassocks, or for rugs. It consists of a short, upright stitch.

HOLBEIN STITCH (DOUBLE RUNNING STITCH A simple, reversible running stitch most commonly used in blackwork embroidery and Assisi embroidery. Named after Hans Holbein the Younger, a 16th century portrait painter best known for his paintings of Henry VII and his children, almost all of whom are depicted wearing clothing decorated with blackwork embroidery.

KNOTTED STITCHES Stitches used to give a definite texture. They can be detached points, or knots close together, or knots made as an addition to another stitch. Stitches in this group include; Armenian edging, braid edging, bullion or bullion knot (caterpillar, coil, grub, knot point de rose, Porto Rico rose, post, roll, worm, wound) chinese knot, coral, double, Spanish (teardrop)

tied, zigzag, dot (simple dot), double knot (Danish knot, Old English knot, Palestrina, Smyrna, tied coral), fourlegged knot, French knot (French dot, knotted, twisted knot, wound knot), knotted buttonhole, knotted cable, knotted chain, knotted feather, knotted stem, tailor's buttonhole.

LINE STITCH (DOUBLE RUNNING STITCH, DOUBLE RUNNING EMBROIDERY) One of the oldest, simplest, and most effective counted-thread stitches. The basis of blackwork, it can be made to follow any outline except curves. Equally spaced running stitches are made, and the space between them is filled on the return journey to make a thin line, but it is important that these second stitches go into the same holes as the first; otherwise, the line will not be clear.

LOCK STITCH Made by the majority of domestic sewing machines since the 1860s. Two threads are used; one runs along top of the work, and the other underneath, and they twist around each other and lock together at every stitch. It has the advantage over machine chain stitch in that it is not possible to undo the whole row by pulling one end.

LONG & SHORT STITCH (BRICK STITCH, EMBROIDERY STITCH, FEATHERWORK OR OPUS PLUMARIUM, PLUMAGE STITCH, IRISH STITCH, SHADING STITCH, TAPESTRY SHADING STITCH, LEAF STITCH) Called Opus Plumarium in the Middle Ages, not to be confused with modern featherstitch. The first row of stitches is alternately long and short. The other is all the same length and fits into the first row. It looks best when worked in floss silks or fine crewel wools, and takes variation in color beautifully, being frequently used for shading the petals of flowers.

MOSSOUL STITCH (See HERRINGBONE STITCH) An overlapped "V"-shaped stitch, this pattern consist of rows of parallel lines, which in any two adjacent rows slope in opposite directions.

OPEN-BUTTONHOLE STITCH (BLANKET STITCH) Looped stitch to strengthen the edge of material, and prevent it from raveling.

OPEN-CHAIN STITCH (SQUARE STITCH, SMALL WRITING, LADDER STITCH) Variation of chain stitch, where complete designs on household linens are carried out in it. The name *small writing* comes from the traced or written line, over which the stitch is worked. It is quite like ordinary chain stitch but a little wider, as the needle does not go in at the same place as it came out, but just to the right.

OPENWORK STITCH (PUNCH STITCH) General term for a pierced decoration.

OUTLINE STITCH (See STEM STITCH, CREWEL STITCH) Perfect, versatile stitch for outlining, because it follows curves well.

OVERLAY STITCH (See SPOT STITCH)

PADDING STITCHES Sometimes it is desirable to raise stitches, especially satin stitch, in order to give a little modeling, in which case, another stitch has to be worked first, underneath the main one. The two stitches used as padding are *satin* and *chain*. When satin is used over satin, the two layers are worked at right angles to each other, and this is the method employed in the fine French white-on-white embroidery of the 19th and 20th centuries.

PARIS POINT (See PIN STITCH, POINT DE PARIS, MOCK HEMSTITCH)

PEKINESE STITCH (CHINESE STITCH) A composite stitch with backstitch as its basis. This is worked first, rather large, and then a second thread is laced through the stitches, going forward two and back one. A firm thread is needed for the lace to keep its shape.

PETIT POINT (TENT STITCH) A smaller, usually diagonal tent stitch made on stiff canvas with one foundation thread (in contrast to 2 or more threads of a needlepoint).

PIN STITCH (POINT DE PARIS, PARIS POINT, MOCK HEMSTITCH) Drawn-fabric stitch used to make a decorative join or to apply lace, often in lingerie, which is worked with a thick needle and a fine thread on firm silk or cotton, and relies on the holes so formed to make the decoration. It is not as strong a stitch as point turc and the raw edge must be neatened.

PLUSH STITCH (VELVET STITCH, RUG STITCH, TASSEL STITCH, RAISED STITCH, ASTRAKHAN STITCH) Counted-thread stitch making a series of loops that may be cut or left uncut according to the design. Each loop is held in place by a tent- or cross stitch. It was very popular in the mid-19th century, when sculptured effects in Berlin woolwork were common, and in 17th century panels, it was used to depict fur on costumes and the coats of some animals, in raised or stumpwork embroidery. Plush stitch can also be used for rugs.

PORTUGUESE STITCH (LONG-ARMED CROSS STITCH, LONG-LEGGED CROSS STITCH, PLAITED SLAVE STITCH, PORTUGUESE STITCH) Variation of cross stitch, which is very popular for canvas work (needlepoint), especially for small articles such as church hassocks, as it is very strong. It is also used in needle-made rugs. The first diagonal stitch of the cross, upwards from left to right, is twice the length of the second arm of the cross, and so a plaited effect is obtained. Unlike cross stitch, where it is possible to work the first half of each stitch all along a row and then return, each long-armed cross must be finished before the next is started.

PUNCH STITCH (FOUR-SIDED STITCH, OPEN GROUNDWORK, OPENWORK STITCH, SINGLE FAGGOT STITCH) Drawn fabric stitch that may either be used in a single line to form a decorative join or to apply lace, or (worked in a different way) as a filling stitch. It consists of a series of joined squares and can be worked on a firm fabric with a thick needle and fine thread, or on loosely woven scrim or linen when used as a filling. Punch stitch makes a very strong joining stitch and surplus fabric can be cut away. (Used in Rhodes work or punch work.)

PUNTO Italian word for stitch, and used the same way as the French word point. It means a stitch made in needlepoint lace, but in various forms of cutwork which were the antecedents of lace, punto is used with another word to describe early techniques; for example, *punto tagliato* (cutwork), *punto tirato* (drawn threadwork), and *punto in aria* (needlepoint lace).

RICE STITCH (CROSSED CORNERS CROSS STITCH) Variation of cross stitch, much used in modern canvas work and needlepoint, which is important for its texture, and because it covers the ground completely. First, a series of large cross-stitches covering four threads of canvas is made, then each arm of each cross is crossed, sometimes with a different thickness or color of thread.

ROCOCO STITCH Counted-thread stitch very popular in the 17th century and revived in the late-19th century. It consists of small bundles of stitches drawn together with holes between each bundle. A straight stitch is made over two threads of ground fabric, and tied down from right to left, taking in the right hand vertical thread of fabric, then three similar stitches are made over the same threads, the tying stitch for the left hand one taking in the left hand vertical thread. Continued alternately up and down, working from right to left.

ROMANIAN STITCH (JANINA STITCH, FIGURE STITCH, ORIENTAL COUCHING, ANTIQUE COUCHING) Couched stitch consisting of a thread taken across the design and then crossed by a small stitch in the center. The angle of this crossing stitch and the number of times the laid thread is crossed make for the variety of names. For example,

Romanian stitch has one cross at a slight angle. Romanian couching has several crosses at the same angle. Oriental couching and figure stitch have such oblique crosses that there is no effect of a marked line.

RUNNING STITCH (STRAIGHT STITCH) The stitch involves inserting the needle into a fabric and taking it out at small intervals. The most basic of hand sewing stitches, from garment-making to embroidery.

SATIN STITCH (GEOMETRICAL SATIN STITCH, SURFACE STITCH, SHAM SATIN STITCH) Very simple stitch consisting of taking the thread over and over from one edge to the other of a design in close parallel lines, keeping it perfectly smooth and even so that it resembles satin.

SLIP STITCH OR BLIND STITCH Used to hold down a hem where it is important that the stitches show as little as possible on the right side. A single thread is picked up with the needle on the main fabric and then the needle slides along and takes up a small piece of the fold. Not a strong stitch but a most useful one in dressmaking and plain sewing.

SMYRNA STITCH (DOUBLE-CROSS STITCH, STAR STITCH) Thick stitch that can be worked in two different threads and colors. A diagonal cross stitch veering two threads vertically and horizontally is worked and then covered by an upright cross-stitch to give a star effect.

SPLIT STITCH Because it looks like a chain stitch, split stitch is put into that group, but it is unique, as it depends on being worked with a soft, untwisted silk thread that can be split with the needle. It can be used for very fine line work or as a fine-filling stitch, and was used extensively for depicting hands and faces in the opus anglicanum of the Middle Ages.

SQUARE-CHAIN STITCH (OPEN-CHAIN STITCH, ROMAN-CHAIN STITCH, LADDER STITCH) Worked in the same way as a chain stitch, but the needle is inserted diagonally from the right hand side of the row of stitches to the left. It is always worked downward and has the appearance of a ladder-depending on how widely the stitches are worked.

SQUARE STITCH An off-loom bead weaving stitch that mimics the appearance of beadwork created on a loom. Because each bead in a square is connected by thread to each of the four beads surrounding it, this is a strong stitch.

STAB STITCH Short running stitch used on thick materials including leather, made by stabbing the needle straight down though the material and straight up a little farther along.

STEM STITCH (See CREWEL STITCH, OUTLINE STITCH, STALK STITCH, SOUTH KENSINGTON STITCH) One of the most frequently used outline stitches, forming a continuous line of overlapped stitches. The stitch is typically used to make narrow stems and veins of leaves.

TENT STITCH (PETIT POINT) A plain diagonal stitch going over one or more threads of the ground fabric, usually canvas.

UNDERSIDE COUCHING Method of couching metal threads, generally used in the opus anglicanum of the Middle Ages, in which no tying-down thread is visible. The couching thread, of well-waxed linen, is underneath the work and is brought to the surface at regular intervals to encircle the metal thread, and is put back through the same hole as it came up. With a sharp tug, a tiny loop of metal thread is pulled down to the back and held there. The secret of this technique had been lost until, at the beginning of this century, it was rediscovered by Louis de Farcy (1841-1921) who called it *point couche, rentre ou retire*. This method makes for much longer wear than surface couching, as in goldwork it is usually the couching threads that give way, leaving the strands of metal threads loose.

VELVET STITCH (See PLUSH STITCH)

WHITEWORK Term referring to any embroidery worked in white thread on a white ground, but especially to muslin embroidery, Ayrshire embroidery, *broderie anglaise* (eyelet embroidery), Madeira work, Renaissance embroidery, and Richelieu embroidery.

STOLE
A narrow piece of fabric, frequently embroidered, that is worn around the shoulders of a priest officiating at the service of the Eucharist. A deacon wears the stole over his left shoulder. The garment is derived from a linen handkerchief or napkin, which had to be carried on the shoulder, as in ancient Greece and Rome there were no pockets. Ecclesiastical stoles were originally embroidered along their entire length, but in the 19th and 20th centuries it was considered sufficient to work a small panel above the fringed ends and a cross, center-back, over the seam.

STRAPWORK
Style of ornament in vogue in the 15th and 16th centuries, consisting of interlacing bands. It was used in woodwork (staircases, chairs, beds), plasterwork, and metalwork, as well as embroidery, and can often be seen in the patterning on costumes of both men and women in 16th-century portraits. It was carried out by the sewing down of braid or by stitches and possibly jewels outlining the strap shapes.

STRIÉ
A very fine, irregular streaked effect made by a slight variance in the color of warp yarns. Origin: French—streaked.

STUART
In English history it is the period between 1603, when James VI of Scotland (James Stuart) became James I of England, and 1714, when Queen Anne dies, thus generally taken to mean the 17th century. The period was interrupted by the Commonwealth (1649-1660), when such frivolities as embroidery were frowned upon by the Puritan element in the country. They forbade the representation of the Life of Christ or any New Testament subjects as idolatry. For this reason, many 17th century needleworks show scenes from the Old Testament, but never the New Testament. The other type of work known at this time is crewelwork, and it was usually made into large hangings.

STUMP WORK
(See RAISED WORK)

SUZANI
A type of embroidered and decorative tribal textile made in Tajikistan, Uzbekistan, Kazakhstan, and other Central Asian countries. Suzani is from the Persian word *Suzan*, which means needle. Suzanis were traditionally made by Central Asian women as a dowry gift to impress a future husband and his family, and used to decorate the home, especially on the wedding day. In the 20th century, Soviet control in Uzbekistan forbade handcrafts, and ridiculed native clothing styles to promote modern Russian fashions. After the collapse of the Soviet Union in 1991, this important form of needlework has become very popular, and now suzanis are made in workshops as well as in the home. They can be hand- as well as machine-stitched in satin or chain stitch.

SWAG
A festoon of imitation drapery or a garland of flowers, fruit, or leaves. A popular Neoclassical ornament.

## TABBY WEAVE
Most common of all weaves, sometimes called plain weave, consisting of warp threads interlaced with weft threads in a regular over-and-under sequence, with the return row being under and over.

## TAMBOUR
Frame shaped like a drum, on which the embroidery known as tambouring was done. The original frames consisted of two hoops of wood, one fitting into the other, between which the fabric to be worked was stretched. The hoops were mounted on a curved wooden base that rested on the lap. Later this base was discarded, and the hoops were mounted on a stand, which might have a reel, underneath, where the continuous thread was wound, or else they were fixed to a clamp that fastened to a table.

## TAPESTRY
An intricate weave employing several sets of heavy filler yarns on a single warp that produces a multi-colored pattern. Originally made with large-scale scenic designs that frequently illustrated a story. They were used as decorative wall hangings but also provided insulation. Greek origin: *tap'es*—rug.

## TAFFETA
A plain weave that is reversible, because the same-size yarns are used for the warp and filler. The firm construction is lightweight, which gives the resulting fabric a crisp hand. Origin: Persian, *taftan*—to twist.

## TINSEL
Originally, ornamentation on fabric in gold and silver in the form of threads, spangles, or strips that made the fabric sparkle. Later the word became more applicable to the sparkle than to the precious metal. Now, tinsel means a flattened copper wire of various widths and thicknesses electroplated to give it a silver, gold, or other colored surface. Also, anything that glitters.

## TOILE
A refined cotton or linen print, usually monochrome, with intricately detailed pattern. Designs originally etched on copper rollers often depicted bucolic or rustic settings.

## TOILE DE JOUY
Printed fabric made at Jouy in France by Philippe Oberkampf from 1760 to 1815. They were usually printed on white or off-white grounds in monotone red, blue, green, or black.

## TRAPUNTO
(STUFF QUILTING)
A type of quilting in which quilted designs stand in high relief against a lower background. Single stitches outline the pattern. A slit is made in the fabric layer on the back of the quilted material and fiber batting is inserted to pad each section of the design to be raised.

## TREFOIL
A Gothic decorative motif with three lobes, instead of four, like the quatrefoil.

## TURKEY
For many centuries, Turkey was at the center of the powerful Ottoman Empire, and is equally poised between East and West on some of the oldest trade routes in the world. So the Turks have had access to the best silks, both threads and fabrics, from Persia and India as well as those produced at Constantinople from the 7th century, and also to metal threads, Indian cotton and Egyptian linen. Being mainly a Moslem country, its designs show stylized plants and foliage and swirling curves, with few human and animal figures. Embroidery is worked on many domestic articles such as towels, hangings, cushion covers, women's costumes and especially mantles.

## TUSSAH
A rough silk extruded from the cocoons of uncultivated silkworms. Slubs appear in the yarn as it is spun, which leaves an uneven depth of color, especially after dyeing. Fabric woven with tussah will have an uneven surface.

## TWILL
A basic weave where the filler threads pass over two or more ends in a regular progression. Creating a diagonal pattern. Origin: Scotland, *twill*—to make a diagonal effect.

## UNION CLOTH
A cloth most often used for printing that is woven with blended yarns. The filler is usually twisted linen and cotton, and the warp is generally cotton.

## VALENCE
Hanging drapery attached to a canopy, altar, top of a window frame, or bed (both from the tester and the frame). Generally they are gathered, pleated, formed into swags, or otherwise decorated with tassels or braid.

## VELVET
A plush fabric with a surface that is a short, thick pile. This is manufactured by weaving two cloths face to face simultaneously, which are then cut apart by the shuttle knife as they come off the loom.

## VELVET WORK
Embroidery on velvet is difficult because of the pile. When the fabric has been enriched, as for church vestments, it has been usual to work suitable motifs on linen and apply them to the velvet, putting only a few connecting stitches or tendrils onto the fabric itself. In the late-19th century, however, Caulfield and Saward (1882) suggested two other types of velvet embroidery: Outlining the pattern on raised or embossed velvet in silk or gold thread, and marking any veins or flower centers of the design in silk with crewel, or long, satin stitches; applying velvet to silk by pasting linen or holland to the back of the velvet, and cutting out shapes and sewing them onto the silk; adding gold or silk outlines is also called velvet work.

## VENETIAN CUTWORK
(ROMAN CUTWORK)
Popular late-19th century form of cutwork, done on strong, washable fabrics. The outline of the design is worked in close buttonholing, with the edge of the stitch on the outside of the design. The fabric between the buttonhole lines is then cut away and the spaces filled with bars and wheel. It resembles Richelieu and Renaissance embroidery.

## VESTMENTS
Generally refers to a set of ritual garments worn by clergy at the Eucharist service. It also refers to a complete set of furnishings for priest, assistants, and place of worship.

## VENICE GOLD
Gold thread imported into England by the Venetian traders in the 16th and 17th centuries.

## VICTORIAN
The period in British history that spanned the long reign of Queen Victoria, from 1837 to 1901. This mechanized sewing-machine era saw far-reaching changes during this time, and revolutionized both domestic and commercial sewing. Berlin work, *broidery anglaise* or eyelet embroidery were the most popular methods. William Morris and his associates had a tremendous influence on matters of taste and craft work.

## VOIDED
A word describing part of a design where the pattern is defined by what is left unworked, rather than by what is put in, as in some stencilling techniques. Many Oriental embroideries make use of this technique, and Assisi embroidery is another example of where the design is voided, with only the background being worked.

## VOLUTE
A motif that depicts a spiral scroll or coil inspired by ram's horns.

## WARP
Threads of a woven textile that run vertically through the loom.

## WEFT
Horizontal yarns of a woven textile.

## WOAD
A natural blue dyestuff used in Europe and Britain since ancient times. Until the introduction of indigo from India in the 16th century, it was the most important blue dye in these countries. It was prepared by fermenting the leaves of the woad plant, *Isatis tinctoria*. and was used chiefly on wool.

## WOOL
The fiber made from the fleece of sheep, goats, and alpaca. Noted for its durability, breathability, and warmth. Wool fibers vary in crimp, length, and thickness, and are good insulators.

## YARN DYED
Cloth that is woven with yarns that have been dyed prior to weaving. Most good-quality fabrics are yarn dyed.

## ZARI EMBROIDERY
Type of north Indian work that covers the ground fabric almost entirely with metal thread, spangles, and jewels. Now it is done only for the tourist trade and sold on small articles such as caps, belts, and evening bags. It is said that the most exquisite example of Zari work ever to be prepared was a carpet made for the Maharaja of Baroda and exhibited at the Delhi Art Exhibition of 1902–03. This was worked entirely with seed pearls, large-size pearls, diamonds, and rubies, and was stitched together with gold wires.

# Index

## Sources

WHERE TO FIND B.VIZ
DESIGN CREATIONS:

bviz.com

Annelle Primos
Jackson, Mississippi
aprimos.com

Bremermann Design
New Orleans, Louisiana
bremermanndesign.com

Cal-a-Vie Antiques
Vista, California
antiques.calavie.com

Coleman Taylor Textiles
Montgomery, Alabama
colemantaylortextiles.com

Fireside Antiques
Baton Rouge, Louisiana
firesideantiques.com

Foxglove Antiques
Atlanta, Georgia
foxgloveantiques.com

Indulge Décor
Houston, Texas
indulgedecor.com

Iris & Company
Birmingham, Alabama
irisandcompany.com

The Mews
Dallas, Texas
themews.net

Segreto Finishes
Houston, Texas
segretofinishes.com

Social, A Shop for Gracious Living
Memphis, Tennessee
901.766.6746

Watkins Culver
Houston, Texas
watkinsculver.com

## Bibliography

Clabburn, Pamela. *The Needleworker's Dictionary*, William Morrow and Company, 1976.

Coleman, Brian D. *Fortuny Interiors*, Gibbs Smith, 2012.

Denny, Walter B., Sumru Belger Krody. *The Sultan's Garden: The Blossoming of Ottoman Art*, HALI Publications Limited, 2012 (Published in conjunction with exhibition of the same name at the Textile Museum in Washington, DC).

De Osma, Guillermo. *Fortuny: The Life and Work of Mariano Fortuny*, Rizzoli International Publications, 1980.

Deschodt, Anne-Marie, Doretta Davanzo Poli. *Fortuny*, Harry N. Abrams, Inc., 2001.

Hardouin-Fugier, Bernard Berthod, Martine Chavent-Fusaro., Editions de l'Amateur 1994.

Harvy, Janet. *Traditional Textiles of Central Asia*, Thames & Hudson Ltd, 1996.

IPEK: *Imperial Ottoman Silks and Velvets*, Azimuth Editions Limited on behalf of TEB Iletisim ve Yayincilik a.s., 2001.

Meller, Susan. Silk and Cotton: *Textiles from the Central Asia That Was*, Abrams, New York, 2013.

Park, Molly, Jennifer Park. *Fortuny Y Madrazo: An Artistic Legacy Queen Sofia Spanish Institute*, 2012.

Riffel, Melanie, Sophie Rouart, Marc Walter. *Toile de Jouy: Printed Textiles in the Classic French Style*, Thames and Hudson Ltd., 2003.

Riley, Noel. *The Elements of Design: A Practical Encyclopedia of the Decorative Arts from the Renaissance to the Present*, Octopus Publishing Group Ltd., a division of Simon & Schuster, 2003.

Sadelik, Zamansiz. *Timeless Simplicity*: Gonül Paksoy, Rezan Has Muzesi, 2007.

Stearns, Martha Genung. Bonanza Books, a division of Crown Publishers Inc. by arrangement with Charles Scribner's Sons, 1968.

Stoeltie, Barbara, René Stoeltie. *Paper Illusions: The Art of Isabelle de Borchgrave*, Harry N. Abrams, Inc. 2008.

Sumner, Christina. Guy Petherbridge. *Bright Flowers, Textiles and Ceramics of Central Asia*, Powerhouse Publishing in association with Lund Humphries, 2004 (Published in conjunction with the Exhibition Bright Flowers: Textiles and Ceramics of Central Asia at the Powerhouse Museum in Sydney, Australia).

Synge, Lanto. *Art of Embroidery: History of Style and Technique*, The Royal School of Needlework, 2001.

Taylor, Roderick. *Ottoman Embroidery*, Interlink Books, an imprint of Interlink Publishing Group, Inc., 1993.

Tortora, Phyllis G., Robert S. Merkel. *Fairchild's Dictionary of Textiles*, 7th Edition, Queens College of the City University of New York, 1996.

Watson, William Wade. *High Water, High Cotton, High Times*, Dorrance Publishing Company, 2007.

## Dedication and Thank You

To the love of my life and my center of gravity, Michael, thank you for loving me through all my shenanigans—though I love you more. And thank you for always encouraging me and having the patience of your dad, Saint Tony Vizard.

To my children, Sarah and Ross, for hunting antique textiles with the same intensity you formerly hunted Easter eggs, and for being such great kids while being dragged all over creation. Had you been brats, my business would never have gotten this far. My capacity for love square-rooted when you both were born.

I appreciate my departed mother, Ruth Watson, right, for instilling in me the love of travel and learning. And for teaching me to speak properly and not letting me chew gum. To my dad Bill (Touchdown) and Katie Watson for always being there for the kids when we were traveling. And thanks, TD, for turning down my loan, turning up my struggle, and making me more creative. I am also grateful for all my friends and family who have encouraged, recommended, and supported me.

To Belinda Prudhomme, the glue that holds me together, this could have never been done without you, nor would it have been as fun. From nurturing the children while I was building the business to now being my right-hand everything. Your integrity, organization, and intelligence inspire me daily. To Monica Peri and Brenda Farris, I am so grateful for your exceptional talent, patience, and millions of stitches.

To my wonderful hot-blooded Italian mentor, Marina Tosini. Thank you for taking me on many fun European adventures, sharing lots of laughs, and still finding treasures for me in your 90's.

Thank you to Janice Langrall for all your advice and for leading me to Suzanne Slesin, the brilliant ball of publishing passion behind Pointed Leaf Press.

Stafford Cliff, Oh My! You are beyond smart and creative. You are a delightful magician. To Antoine Bootz, you have done more than just take beautiful photographs for the book, you have made me love the look of winter at Locustland, which I did not appreciate before. To all of you at Pointed Leaf Press, Kelly, Frederico, Nick, Beth, Peter, and Marion, thank you for keeping me calm and taking care of so many loose ends.

Gerrie Bremermann, thank you for being the first, starting in 1994, to spread our pillows throughout your wonderful design projects and gorgeous storefront on Magazine Street.

Thank you to Kathryn Brookshire Brown, Todd Moore, and Colleen Scully, who helped me so much in the early days. To Karen Carroll, the first editor to publish my pillows at *Southern Accents* and get the ball rolling. And to *Architectural Digest*, *Elle Decor*, *Flower Magazine*, *Garden and Gun*, *House Beautiful*, *Milieu Magazine*, *Traditional Home*, *Veranda*, and *World of Interiors*, thank you for showing the world our special jewels.

For the many blog posts and social media comments I have seen that highlight our creations, thank you so much. And to George, Cote de Texas, Have Some Decorum, Goop, Peak of Chic, Pigtown Design, Quintessence, Stylecourt, The Scout Guide, What is James Wearing?

A special thanks goes to all the many interior designers and customers who have placed my pillows all over the world. And thank you to all the designers and photographers who shared the projects we included in this book, to Candi Head, for her incredible photograph of the cotton harvest on page 23, and Amy Dixon for the cotton painting and entrepreneurial wisdom while painting socks. To Ann Connelly, thank you for being the ultimate traveling partner.

Thank you Chesie Breen, Ellen Niven and Morgan McLean for keeping me organized and on track.

Last but not least, to Newell Turner and Julia Reed, whose small town Delta backgrounds with big town successes have inspired me for years.

**REBECCA VIZARD, ST. JOSEPH, LOUISIANA, MAY 2015**

### CAPTIONS

**COVER AND BACK COVER** An intricately stitched gold metallic embroidery salvaged from a late-19th century Turkish *bohça* is about to be hand-stitched to a rich wedgwood blue velvet to create the front of a pillow. On the back is a reverse fragment of an appliqué.

**ENDPAPERS** The delicate calligraphy on the back of an antique cloth of gold appliqué shows there is much more than meets the eye in a B.Viz Design pillow.

**OPPOSITE HALF TITLE** A 16th century European appliqué and embroidery with gold-metallic couched cording is too fragile to be made into a pillow, so will be framed for conservation.

**HALF TITLE** These elements will eventually be used to embellish pillows. The circle with the fleur de lys is from a religious vestment. The gold embroidered letters are for brides who want their new initials on a wonderful ring-bearer pillow.

**TITLE PAGES** A typical smattering of antique textile elements and tools of the trade usually crowd my design table. The beautiful calligraphy on the backs of the flower appliqués is a delightful surprise when disassembling a worn textile. Belinda's talented hands are seen with a 19th-century couched cloth of gold appliqué.

**PAGES 4–5** Fallen oak leaves bespeckle the pea gravel at Locustland, and mimic the feel of a drawer full of vining raised embroidery. The lengthy trail of embroidered flowers and leaves from a late-Ottoman Empire caftan will serve to make several long pillows for the middle of a sofa or bed.

**PAGES 6–7** The bark of the majestic live oak in the garden echoes the texture of a French 1920s metallic appliqué.

**PAGES 8–9** My view of Lake Bruin with the colors of winter has inspired the subtle hues of some of my favorite pillows. Moisture-swollen cypress tree trunks and spindly bare limbs feel like a Dutch Master etching.

**PAGE 10** The dock houses our boats. With one flick of a switch they are lowered into the water and ready for cruising.

**PAGE 11** I love Fortuny so much I make even jackets out of the legendary fabric. I wear them anywhere from European cocktail parties to the dock at Lake Bruin.

**PAGES 12–13** The many patinas of the antique and metallic galóns have taken years for me to collect. They are instrumental in the refinement of my pillow compositions.

**OPPOSITE** The Locustland pecan orchard, which was planted by my grandfather, provides pecans for everything from salads and snacks to cookies and pies. The irregular pattern on the shells remind me of Uzbek ikat weavings.

Unless noted below, all photographs are by Antoine Bootz. Every effort has been made to locate copyright holders; any omissions will be corrected in future printings.

16, 133, bottom row right: Dominick Santise, Jr.; 17, 26: Rebecca Vizard; 58: Private Collection The Stapleton Collection/Bridgeman Images; 88: ©National Portrait Gallery, London; 90: Susan Meller, SILK and COTTON: Textiles from the Central Asia that was, Abrams, NY 2013 (Photograph by John McCutcheon); 95, 101, 107, 113, 119, 125, 133, except for top row right and bottom row right: Belinda Prudhomme; 96: ©Marzolino; 108: ©Everett Historical; 114: ©Chronicle/Alamy; 120: ©Ivy Close Images/Alamy; 126: Universal History Archive/UIG/Bridgeman Images; 133, top row right: John Gruen; 134: ©The Mass Gallery, London/Bridgeman Images; 136: Photograph by Mali Azima; 137, 170-171: Photograph by Francesco Lagnese; 138-139, 141, 152, 161, 164, 165: Tria Giovan Photography; 140: Roger Davies/Trunk Archive; 142: Photograph by Erik Kvalsvik; 143: Photograph by Edward Addeo; 144: Tom Beck/Beck Photographic; 145: Photograph by James Patterson; 146, 158-159, 160: Photograph by Peter Vitale; 147, 150, 154, 166: Photograph by Kerri McCaffety; 148, 169: Photograph by Susan Sully; 149: Photograph by Thibault Jeanson; 151: Photograph by John Gruen; 153: Fran Brennan Photography; 155: Simon Upton ©The World of Interiors; 156-157: Photograph by William Waldron; 162-163: Courtesy of Duane Modern; 167: Courtesy of Scott Sanders; 168: Photograph by James Patterson; 172-173: Photograph by Frances Janisch.

B.Viz Design
P.O. Box 646
St. Joseph, Louisiana 71366
(318) 766-4950
www.bviz.com
rebecca@bviz.com
©2015 Rebecca Vizard

Pointed Leaf Press, LLC
Editorial Director: Suzanne Slesin
Design: Stafford Cliff
Production: Dominick J. Santise, Jr.
Editorial Associate: Kelly Koester

Pointed Leaf Press is pleased to offer special discounts for our publications. We also create special edition copies and can provide signed copies upon request. Please contact info@pointedleafpress.com for details or visit our website at www.pointedleafpress.com.

Printed and bound in Italy
First edition
10 9 8 7 6 5 4 3 2
Library of Congress Control Number: 2015943204
ISBN: 978-1-938461-27-9